He That
Is Spiritual

Books by Lewis Sperry Chafer

He That Is Spiritual
A classic on the Christian's relation to the Holy Spirit.

Salvation
A handbook on the cross, salvation, and security.

Grace
An enlightening study of the heart of Christianity.

Satan
Expositions of his origin, purpose, and program.

True Evangelism
Sane, Scriptural methods for the church's great task.

Systematic Theology
An 8-volume comprehensive and unabridged study of the
teachings of Holy Scripture.

Major Bible Themes
a manual of Christian doctrine.

6307p

He That Is Spiritual

A Classic Study of the Biblical Doctrine of Spirituality

by

LEWIS SPERRY CHAFER, D.D., LITT. D.

Former President of Dallas Theological Seminary,
Dallas, Texas
Former Professor of Systematic Theology
Former Editor of *Bibliotheca Sacra*

ZONDERVAN®

GRAND RAPIDS, MICHIGAN 49530 USA

ZONDERVAN.COM/
AUTHORTRACKER

ZONDERVAN®

He That Is Spiritual
Copyright © 1918 by Lewis Sperry Chafer
Revised edition copyright © 1967 by Zondervan

Requests for information should be addressed to:
Zondervan, *Grand Rapids, Michigan 49530*

ISBN-10: 0-310-22341-5
ISBN-13: 978-0-310-22341-2

Printed in the   4 3395 00007 156 6

14 15 16 17 QG 80 79 78 77 76 75 74 73 72

FOREWORD

No subject was more dear to the heart of Dr. Lewis Sperry Chafer than the teaching of the Scriptures on the spiritual life. His own personal devotion to the Lord, so evident to all who knew him, reflected the power of the Holy Spirit in his own life. For him, proper spiritual adjustment to the indwelling Holy Spirit was the divinely designed norm and made possible the lovely fruit of the Spirit described in Galatians 5:22-23. In his twenty-eight years as President of Dallas Theological Seminary he always began the school year with a week of lectures on the basic requirement for effective seminary study found in yielding to the Holy Spirit. Only to spiritually minded students could God reveal the Scriptures, empower for holy living, and provide inner peace and joy.

The twentieth century has witnessed growing interest in the doctrine of the Holy Spirit. The advent of crisis theology with its claim to supernatural revelation has tended to focus attention on the doctrine of the Holy Spirit. In contemporary discussion it has become increasingly apparent that the spiritual life, realized by the filling of the Spirit, is not only the key to spiritual enjoyment and holiness, but also is the profound basis of Biblical epistomology, God's method of revealing spiritual truth to prepared hearts and minds.

In contemporary theology where supernatural revelation by the Holy Spirit is being challenged by the "God is dead" philosophy, and Biblical standards of holiness are confronted by the "new morality," it is refreshing to review the timeless principles provided in the grace of God for a dynamic spiritual life of holiness, peace, and enjoyment.

The republication of these vital teachings which left the pen of its author almost fifty years ago is in itself a testimony to the important truths contained in these pages.

JOHN F. WALVOORD
President, Dallas Theological Seminary

Dallas, Texas

ORIGINAL AUTHOR'S PREFACE

The importance of the subject of this book is beyond estimation. True spirituality is that quality of life in the child of God which satisfies and glorifies the Father. It brings celestial joy and peace to the believer's own heart. Upon it all Christian service depends. Since God purposes to work through human means, the fitness of the instrument determines the progress made.

There is general agreement that the daily life of Christians should be improved; but improvement cannot be had other than in God's way. Merely to exhort an unspiritual Christian is a loss of time and energy. When that Christian becomes spiritual, he will need no exhortation; but himself becomes an exhorter both by precept and example. Christians, as a whole, are satiated with ideals. Their real difficulty is stated in the words: "How to perform that which is good, I find not." The divine way to sufficiency and efficiency must be understood and acted upon, else we fail.

The Bible doctrine concerning the Christian's nature and daily practice, and the relation of these to the death of Christ, is subject to some disagreement. It is not the primary purpose of this book to correct details of doctrine. The object has been rather to state the outstanding revelation of the divine provision for the overcoming life. May we be delivered from controversy over secondary things in the face of our present failure to "walk as it becometh saints."

It is my prayer that this statement of the fact and force of the spiritual life may be helpful to those who are called upon to manifest Christ to a dying world, and who hope to hear the Master say, "Well done."

LEWIS SPERRY CHAFER

CONTENTS

CHAPTER I

CHAPTER II

CHAPTER III

THE FILLING OF THE SPIRIT, OR TRUE SPIRITUALITY

CHAPTER IV

"GRIEVE NOT THE HOLY SPIRIT"

The First Condition of True Spirituality

CHAPTER V

"QUENCH NOT THE SPIRIT"

The Second Condition of True Spirituality

CHAPTER VI

"WALK IN THE SPIRIT"

The Third Condition of True Spirituality

CHAPTER VII

AN ANALOGY AND THE CONCLUSION

He That Is Spiritual

CHAPTER 1

THREE CLASSES OF MEN

THERE IS AN OBVIOUS difference in the character and quality of the daily life of Christians. This difference is acknowledged and defined in the New Testament. There is also a possible improvement in the character and quality of the daily life of many Christians. This improvement is experienced by all such Christians who fulfil certain conditions. These conditions, too, form an important theme in the Word of God.

The Apostle Paul, by the Spirit, has divided the whole human family into three groups: (1) The "natural man," who is unregenerate, or unchanged spiritually; (2) the "carnal man," who is a "babe in Christ," and walks "as a man"; and (3) the "spiritual" man. These groups are classified by the Apostle according to their ability to understand and receive a certain body of Truth, which is of things "*revealed*" unto us by the Spirit. Men are vitally different one from the other as regards the fact of the new birth and the life of power and blessing; but their classification is made evident by their attitude toward things revealed.

In I Corinthians 2:9 to 3:4 this threefold classification is stated. The passage opens as follows: "But as it is written, Eye hath not seen, nor ear heard, neither have entered into the heart of man, the things which God hath prepared for them that love him. But God hath revealed them unto us by his Spirit." A distinction is here drawn between those general subjects of human knowledge which are received through the eye-gate, the ear-gate, or the "heart" (the power to reason), and other subjects which are said to have been "*revealed*" unto us by His Spirit. There is no reference here to any revelation other than that which is already

15

contained in the Scriptures of Truth, and this revelation is boundless, as the passage goes on to state: "For the Spirit [who reveals] searcheth all things, yea, the deep things of God."

Men are classified according to their ability to understand and receive the "deep things of God." Into these "deep things of God" no unaided man can go. "For what man knoweth the things of a man, save the spirit of man which is in him? even so the things of God knoweth no man, but the Spirit of God" (knows them). An unaided man may enter freely into the things of his fellow man because of "the spirit of man which is in him." He cannot extend his sphere. He cannot know experimentally the things of the animal world below him, and certainly he cannot enter a higher sphere and know experimentally the things of God. Even though man, of himself, cannot know the things of God, the Spirit knows them, and a man may be so related to the Spirit that he too may know them. The passage continues: "Now we have received, not the spirit of the world, but the Spirit which is of God; that we may know the things [the "deep things of God," which eye hath not seen, etc.] that are freely given us of God." "We [that is, all saved, excluding none] have received the Spirit which is of God." Here is a great potentiality. Being so vitally related to the Spirit of God as to have Him abiding within, it is possible, because of that fact, to come to know "the things that are freely given to us of God." We could never know them of ourselves: the Spirit knows, He indwells, and He reveals.

This divine revelation is transmitted to us in "words" which the Holy Spirit teacheth, as the Apostle goes on to state: "Which things also we speak, not in the words which man's wisdom teacheth, but which the Holy Spirit teacheth; comparing spiritual things with spiritual." God's Book is a Book of *words* and the very words which convey "man's wisdom" are used to convey things which "eye hath not seen, nor ear heard, neither have entered into the heart of man." Nevertheless unaided man cannot understand these "deep things of God," though couched in words most familiar to man, except as they are *"revealed"* by the Spirit. Just so, in coming to know these revealed things, progress is made only as one spiritual thing is compared with another spiritual thing. Spiritual things must be communicated by spiritual means. Apart from the Spirit there can be no spiritual understanding.

THE NATURAL MAN

"But the natural man receiveth not the things [the revealed or deep things] of the Spirit of God: for they are foolishness unto him: neither can he know them, because they are spiritually discerned." In this passage the natural man is not blamed for his inability. It is simply an accurate statement of the fact of his limitations. The passage also goes on to assign the exact cause of these limitations. We have just been told that revelation is by the Spirit. It therefore follows that the "natural man" is helpless to understand things revealed because he has not received "the Spirit which is of God." He has received only "the spirit of man which is in him." Though he may, with "man's wisdom," be able to read the words, he cannot receive their spiritual meaning. To him the revelation is "foolishness." He cannot *"receive"* it, or *"know"* it.

The preceding verses of the context (I Corinthians 1:18, 23) have defined a part of the divine revelation which is said to be "foolishness" to the "natural man": "For the preaching of the cross is to them that perish foolishness; but unto us which are saved it is the power of God." "But we preach Christ crucified, unto the Jews a stumbling block, and unto the Greeks [Gentiles] foolishness." Much more than the mere historical fact of the death of Christ is here meant. It is the divine unfolding of redemption through grace and includes all the eternal relationships that are made possible thereby. The moral principles and many of the religious teachings of the Bible are within the range of the capacity of the "natural man." From these sources he may eloquently preach; yea, and most seriously, not even knowing that "the deep things of God" exist.

Satan, in his counterfeit systems of truth, is said to have "deep things" to reveal (Revelation 2:24) and "doctrines of devils" (I Timothy 4:1, 2) which things, on the other hand, are as certainly not received by the true child of God; for it is said, "And a stranger will they not follow, but will flee from him: for they know not the voice of strangers" (John 10:5). Yet the "deep things" of Satan are strangely adapted to the blinded, "natural man" and are, therefore, received by him. Every modern cult is evidence establishing the truthfulness of this statement.

The unsaved man, though educated with all of "man's wisdom," and though religious and attentive, is blind to the gospel (II Corinthians 4:3, 4) and if called upon to formulate a doctrinal statement, will naturally formulate a "new theology" which is so "re-stated" as to omit the real meaning of the cross with its unfolding of the "deep things of God." The cross, as a substitutionary sacrifice for sin, is "foolishness" unto him. His very limitations as a "natural man" demand that this shall be so. Human wisdom cannot help him, for "the world by wisdom knew not God." On the other hand, the boundless "deep things of God" are to be *"freely"* given to the one who has received "the Spirit which is of God." The true child of God *may*, therefore, be taught the divine revelation, having received the Spirit. A trained mind, it may be added, will greatly assist; but apart from the presence of the indwelling Teacher, a trained mind avails nothing in coming to know the spiritual meaning of the revealed things of God.

Measureless evil has arisen through the supposition that because a man is well advanced in the "wisdom of this world," his opinions are of value in spiritual matters. The "natural man," with all his learning and sincerity, will find nothing but "foolishness" in the things which are revealed by the Spirit. The knowledge of science cannot be substituted for the indwelling of, and right relation to, the Holy Spirit of God. Apart from the Spirit there can be no regeneration, and the "deep things of God" are unknowable. When an unregenerate teacher openly rejects the vital saving truths of God's Word, those truths will usually be discredited and discarded by the pupil. This is the colossal blunder of many students in universities and colleges today.

It is too generally assumed that the teacher or preacher who is an authority in some branch or branches of human knowledge is, by virtue of that knowledge, equally capable of discernment in spiritual things. It is not so. An unregenerate person (and who is more assuredly unregenerate than the one who denies the foundation and reality of the new birth?) will always be incapable of receiving and knowing the simplest truths of revelation. God is not a reality to the natural man. "God is not in all his thoughts." The unsaved man is therefore distressed and burdened to dispose of the supernatural. A baseless theory of evolution is his best answer to the problem of the origin of the universe. To the regenerate man, God is real and there is satisfaction and rest in the confidence that God is Creator and Lord of all.

The ability to receive and know the things of God is not attained through the schools, for many who are unlearned possess it while many who are learned do not possess it. It is an ability which is born of the indwelling Spirit. For this reason the Spirit has been given to those who are saved that they might know the things which are freely given to them of God. Yet among Christians there are some who are under limitations because of their carnality. They are unable to receive "meat" because of carnality, rather than ignorance.

There are no divine classifications among the unsaved, for they are all said to be "natural" men. There are, however, two classifications of the saved, and in the text under consideration, the "spiritual" man is named before the "carnal" man and is thus placed in direct contrast with the unsaved. This is fitting because the "spiritual" man is the divine ideal. "HE THAT IS SPIRITUAL" (I Corinthians 2:15) is the normal, if not the usual, Christian. But there is a "carnal" man and he must be considered.

THE CARNAL MAN

The Apostle proceeds in chapter 3:1-4 with the description of the "carnal" man: "And I, brethren, could not speak unto you as unto spiritual, but as unto carnal, even as unto babes in Christ. I have fed you with milk, and not with meat: for hitherto ye were not able to bear it, neither yet now are ye able. For ye are yet carnal: for whereas there is among you envying, and strife, and divisions, are ye not carnal, and walk as men? For while one saith, I am of Paul; and another, I am of Apollos; are ye not carnal?"

Some Christians, thus, are said to be "carnal" because they can receive only the milk of the Word, in contrast to the strong meat; they yield to envy, strife and divisions, and are walking as men, while the true child of God is expected to "walk in the Spirit" (Galatians 5:16), to "walk in love" (Ephesians 5:2), and to "keep the unity of the Spirit" (Ephesians 4:3). Though saved, the carnal Christians are walking "according to the course of this world." They are "carnal" because the flesh is dominating them (See Romans 7:14). A different description is found in Romans 8:5-7. There the one referred to is "in the flesh," and so is unsaved; while a "carnal" Christian is not "in the flesh," but he has the flesh *in him*. "But ye are not in the flesh, but in the Spirit if so be that the Spirit of God dwell in you. Now if any man have not the Spirit of Christ, he is none of his."

The "carnal" man, or "babe in Christ," is not "able to bear" the deep things of God. He is only a babe; but even that, it is important to note, is a height of position and reality which can never be compared with the utter incapacity of the "natural man." The "carnal" man, being so little occupied with true spiritual meat, yields to envy and strife which lead to divisions among the very believers. No reference is made here to the superficial fact of outward divisions or various organizations. It is a reference to envy and strife which were working to sunder the priceless fellowship and love of the saints. Different organizations may often tend to class distinctions among the believers, but it is not necessarily so. The sin which is here pointed out is that of the believer who follows human leaders. This sin would not be cured were all the religious organizations instantly swept from the earth, or merged into one. There were present the "Paulites," the "Cephasites," the "Apollosites" and the "Christ-ites" (cf. 1:12). These were not as yet rival organizations, but divisions within the Corinthian church that grew out of envy and strife. History shows that such divisions end in rival organizations. The fact of division was but the outward expression of the deeper sin of loveless, carnal lives. For a Christian to glory in sectarianism is "baby talk" at best, and reveals the more serious lack of true Christian love which should flow out to *all* the saints. Divisions will fade away and their offense will cease when the believers "have love one for the other."

But the "carnal" Christian is also characterized by a "walk" that is on the same plane as that of the "natural" man. "Are ye not carnal, and walk as men?" (cf. II Corinthians 10:2-5). The objectives and affections are centered in the same unspiritual sphere as that of the "natural" man. In contrast to such a fleshly walk, we read: "This I say then, Walk in the Spirit, and ye shall not fulfil the lust of the flesh." This is spirituality.

THE SPIRITUAL MAN

The second classification of believers in this passage is of the spiritual man. He, too, is proven to be all that he is said to be by one test of his ability to receive and know the divine revelation. "He that is spiritual discerneth all things."

The progressive order of this whole context is evident:

First, the divine revelation is now given. It is concerning things which, "eye hath not seen, nor ear heard, neither have entered into the heart of man." It is revealed by the Spirit (I Corinthians 2:9, 10).

Second, the revelation is of the "deep things of God," which no man can know. However the Spirit knows them (I Corinthians 2:10).

Third, believers have received the Spirit who knows, in order that they too may know the deep things of God (I Corinthians 2:12).

Fourth, the divine wisdom is hidden in the very words of God's Book; but the spiritual content of these words is understood only as one is able to compare spiritual things with spiritual (I Corinthians 2:13).

Fifth, the "natural man" cannot receive the things of the

Spirit of God, for they are foolishness unto him, neither can he know them, because they are only by the Spirit discerned. He has not received the Spirit which is of God (I Corinthians 2:14).

Sixth, a carnal Christian is born again and possesses the indwelling Spirit; but his carnality hinders the full ministry of the Spirit (I Corinthians 3:1-4).

Seventh, "HE THAT IS SPIRITUAL" discerneth all things. There is no limitation upon him in the realm of the things of God. He can "freely" receive the divine revelation and he glories in it. He, too, may enter, as any other man, into the subjects which are common to human knowledge. He discerneth *all* things; yet he is discerned, or understood by no man. How could it be otherwise since he has "the mind of Christ?"

There are two great spiritual changes which are possible to human experience — the change from the "natural" man to the saved man, and the change from the "carnal" man to the "spiritual" man. The former is divinely accomplished when there is a real faith in Christ; the latter is accomplished when there is a real adjustment to the Spirit. Experimentally the one who is saved through faith in Christ, may at the same time wholly yield to God and enter at once a life of true surrender. Doubtless this is often the case. It was thus in the experience of Saul of Tarsus (Acts 9:4-6). Having recognized Jesus as his Lord and Saviour, he also said, "Lord, what wilt thou have me to do?" There is no evidence that he ever turned from this attitude of yieldedness to Christ. However, it must be remembered that many Christians are carnal. To these the word of God gives clear directions as to the steps to be taken that they may become spiritual. There is then a possible change from the carnal to the spiritual state.

The "spiritual" man is the divine ideal in life and ministry, in power with God and man, in unbroken fellowship and blessing. To discover these realities and the revealed conditions upon which all may be realized is the purpose of the following pages.

CHAPTER 2

THE MINISTRIES OF THE SPIRIT

A CHRISTIAN IS A CHRISTIAN because he is rightly related to Christ; but "he that is spiritual" is spiritual because he is rightly related to the Spirit, in addition to his relation to Christ in salvation. It therefore follows that any attempt to discover the fact and conditions of true spirituality must be based upon a clear understanding of the Bible revelation concerning the Spirit in His possible relationships to men. It seems to be the latest device of Satan to create confusion concerning the work of the Spirit, and this confusion appears among the most pious and earnest believers. The quality of the believer's life is a tremendous issue before God, and Satan's power is naturally directed against the purpose of God. Satan's ends could be gained in no better way than to promote some statement of truth that misses the vital issues, or establishes positive error, and thus hinders the right understanding of the divinely provided source of blessing. This general confusion on the Bible teachings regarding the Spirit is reflected in our hymnology. Bible expositors are united in deploring the fact that so many hymns on the Spirit are unscriptural. This confusion is also reflected today in the unbalanced and unbiblical theories which are held by some sects.

THE CHANGING RELATIONSHIPS

It is not within the purpose of this book to undertake a complete statement of the Bible teachings concerning the Spirit of God, but certain aspects of the whole revelation must be understood and received before the God-provided life and walk in the Spirit can be comprehended or intelligently entered into. The Bible teaching concerning the Spirit may be divided into three general divisions: (1) The Spirit according to the Old Testament; (2) The Spirit according to the Gospels and as far in the Scriptures as The Acts 10:43; (3) The Spirit according to the remainder of The Acts and the Epistles.

I. The Spirit According to the Old Testament

Here, as in all the Scriptures, the Spirit of God is declared to be a Person, rather than an influence. He is revealed as being equal in deity and attributes with the other Persons of the Godhead. However, though ceaselessly active in all the centuries before the cross, it was not until after that great event that He became an *abiding* Presence in the hearts of men (John 7:37-39; 14:16, 17). He often came upon people as revealed in the events which are recorded in the Old Testament. He came upon them to accomplish certain objects and left them, when the work was done, as freely as He had come. So far as the record goes, no person in that whole period had any choice, or expected to have any choice, in the sovereign movements of the Spirit. Elisha and David are sometimes thought to be exceptions. It is not at all clear that Elisha's request to Elijah, "let a double portion of thy spirit be upon me," was, in the mind of the young man Elisha, a prayer for the Spirit of God. David did pray that the Spirit should not be taken from him; but this was in connection with his great sin. His prayer was that the Spirit should not depart because of his sin. His confession was before God and the occasion was removed. During the period covered by the Old Testament, the Spirit was related to men in a sovereign way. In the light of subsequent revelation in the New Testament the prayer of David, "and take not thy Holy Spirit from me," cannot reasonably be made now. The Spirit has come to abide.

II. The Spirit According to the Gospels and the Acts to 10:43

The essential character of the Spirit's relation to men during the period of the Gospels is that of transition, or progression, from the age-long relationships of the Old Testament to the final and abiding relationships in this dispensation of grace.

The early instruction of the disciples had been in the Old Testament, and the statement from Christ that the Spirit might be had by asking (Luke 11:13) was so new to them that, so far as the record goes, they never asked. This new relationship, suggested by the statement, "How much more shall your heavenly Father give the Holy Spirit to them that ask him," characterizes a forward step in the progressive relationship of the Spirit with men during the Gospel period.

Just before His death Jesus said: "And I will pray the Father, and he shall give you another Comforter, that he may abide with you for ever; even the Spirit of truth; whom the world cannot receive, because it seeth him not, neither knoweth him: but ye know him; for he dwelleth with you, and shall be in you" (John 14:16, 17). The words, "I will pray," may have suggested to the disciples that they had failed to pray. However, the prayer of the Son of God cannot be unanswered and the Spirit who was *"with"* them was soon to be *"in"* them.

After His resurrection and just before His ascension, Jesus breathed on His disciples and said unto them, "Receive ye the Holy Spirit" (John 20:22). They possessed the indwelling Spirit from that moment; but that relationship was evidently incomplete according to the plan and purpose of God, for He soon "commanded them that they should not depart from Jerusalem, but wait for the promise of the Father, which, saith he, ye have heard of me" (Acts 1:4, cf. Luke 24:49). The "promise of the Father" was of the Spirit, but evidently concerning that yet unexperienced ministry of the Spirit coming *"upon"* them for power.

There was, then, a period, according to the Gospels, when the disciples were without the Spirit as the multitudes of the Old Testament time had been; but they were granted the new privilege of prayer for the presence of the Spirit. Later, the Lord Himself prayed to the Father that the Spirit who was then *with* them might be *in* them to *abide*. He then breathed on them and they received the indwelling Spirit; yet they were commanded not to depart out of Jerusalem. No service could be undertaken and no ministry performed until the Spirit had come *upon* them for power. "Ye shall receive power, after that the Holy Spirit is come upon you: and ye shall be witnesses unto me." This is a revelation of conditions which are abiding. It is not enough that servants and witnesses have received the Spirit: He must come upon them, or fill them.

THE DAY OF PENTECOST

At least three distinct things were accomplished on the Day of Pentecost concerning the relationship of the Spirit with men:

(1) The Spirit made His advent into the world here to abide throughout this dispensation. As Christ is now located at the right hand of God, though omnipresent, so the Spirit, though omnipresent, is now locally abiding in the world, in a temple, or habitation, of living stones (Ephesians 2:19-22). The individual believer is also spoken of as a temple of the Spirit (I Corinthians 6:19). The Spirit will not leave the world, or even one stone of that building until the age-long purpose of forming that temple is finished. The Ephesian passage reads thus: "Now therefore ye are no more strangers and foreigners, but fellow-citizens with the saints, and of the household of God; and are built [being built, into the temple, cf. v. 21] upon the foundation of the apostles and prophets [New Testament prophets, cf. 4:11], Jesus Christ himself being the chief corner stone; in whom all the building fitly framed together groweth unto an holy temple in the Lord: in whom ye also are builded [are being builded] together for an habitation of God through the Spirit."

The Spirit came on the Day of Pentecost and that aspect of the meaning of Pentecost will no more be repeated than the incarnation of Christ. There is no occasion to call the Spirit to "*come*," for He is here.

(2) Again, Pentecost marked the beginning of the formation of a new body, or organism which, in its relation to Christ, is called "the church which is his body." Though the Church had not been mentioned in the Old Testament, Christ had promised

that He would "build" it. "Upon this rock I will build my church" (Matthew 16:18). The Church, as a distinct organism, is not mentioned as in existence until after the advent of the Spirit at Pentecost. It is then stated "And the same day there were added unto them about three thousand souls" (Acts 2:41. While the Greek word for the *church* does not appear in this text, as it does in 2:47, — "And the Lord added to the church daily such as should be saved," the unity which is here being formed is none other than the Church. See also Acts 5:14; 11:24.) According to these passages, the Church, which in the Gospels was yet future, is already brought into existence and to it (the believers united to the Lord), are being added "such as should be saved." It is said that "the Lord was adding to the church." Certainly there is no reference here to a human organization, for no such thing had been formed. It is not a membership created by human voice, for it is the *Lord* who is adding to this Church. A body had begun to be formed of members who were vitally joined to Christ and indwelt by the Spirit and these very facts of relationship made them an organism and united them by ties which are closer than any human ties. To this organism other members were being "added" as they were saved. That formation and subsequent building of the "church which is his body" is the baptism with the Holy Spirit as it is written: "For as the body is one, and hath many members, and all the members of that one body, being many, are one body: so also is Christ. For by one Spirit are we all baptized into one body" (I Corinthians 12:12, 13). Thus the meaning of Pentecost includes, as well, the beginning of the baptizing ministry of the Spirit of God.[1] This ministry is evidently accomplished whenever a soul is saved.

(3) So, also, at Pentecost the lives that were prepared were filled with the Spirit, or the Spirit came *upon* them for power as promised. Thus they began the age-long ministry of witnessing. The mighty effect of this new ministry of the Spirit was especially revealed in the case of Peter. Before, he had cursed and sworn for fear in the presence of a little maid: now he not only fearlessly

---

[1]See also page 38.

accuses the rulers of the Nation of being guilty of the murder of the Prince of Life, but the power of his testimony is seen in the salvation of three thousand souls.

Thus the full meaning of Pentecost was revealed in the advent of the Spirit into the world to abide throughout this dispensation; in the baptism of many members into Christ; and the empowering of those whose lives were prepared for the work of witnessing unto Christ.

A careful student of the Scriptures may distinguish yet one further step in the whole transition from the relationships of the Spirit as revealed in the Old Testament to that which is the final relationship in the present dispensation. Much that has been mentioned thus far is made permanent in this age. The last step here mentioned is in regard to the fact that during the well defined period in which the Gospel was preached to Jews only, which was from Pentecost to Peter's visit to Cornelius, or about eight years, the Spirit, in one case at least, was received through the Jewish rite (Hebrews 6:2) of the laying on of hands (Acts 8:14-17). Though this human rite was continued in a few instances in connection with the *filling* of the Spirit and for service (Acts 6:6; 13:3; 19:6; I Timothy 4:14; II Timothy 1:6), the Spirit was to be received, under the final provisions for this age, by believing on Christ for salvation (John 7:37-39). This final condition for receiving the Spirit began with the preaching of the Gospel to the Gentiles in Cornelius' house (Acts 10:44. cf. Acts 15:7-9, 14) and has continued throughout the age. There is no record that hands were laid on believers in Cornelius' house. The Spirit "fell upon them" (this phrase is evidently synonymous with receiving the Spirit) when they believed (Acts 8:18; 10:43, 44; 11:14, 15). The events in Cornelius' house undoubtedly marked the beginning of a new and abiding order.

III. The Spirit According to the Remainder of the Acts and the Epistles

The final and abiding relationships of the Spirit with men in this age are revealed under seven ministries. Two of these are ministries to the unsaved world; four are ministries to all believers alike; and one is a ministry to all believers who come into right adjustment with God.

THE MINISTRIES OF THE SPIRIT

These seven ministries are:

First, The Ministry of the Spirit in Restraining. The one passage bearing on this aspect of the Spirit's work (II Thessalonians 2:6-8) is not wholly free from disagreement among Bible students. In the passage, the Apostle has just disclosed the fact that, immediately before the return of Christ in His glory, there will be an apostasy and the "man of sin" will be revealed "who opposeth and exalteth himself above all that is called God, or that is worshipped." He then goes on to state: "And now ye know what withholdeth that he might be revealed in his time. For the mystery of iniquity doth already work: only he who now letteth will let, until he be taken out of the way. And then shall that Wicked [one] be revealed, whom the Lord shall consume with the spirit of his mouth, and shall destroy with the brightness of his coming." "The man of sin" must appear with all the power of Satan (v. 9); but he will appear at God's appointed time, — "that he may be revealed in his time," and this will be as soon as a hindering One be gone out of His place. Then shall that wicked one be revealed, whom the Lord shall destroy at His coming.

The name of the restrainer, here referred to, is not revealed. His sovereign power over the earth and all the forces of darkness identifies Him with the Godhead, and since the Spirit is the present active force in this dispensation, it follows that the reference in the passage is to the Spirit of God. Satan might have sufficient power; but hardly would it be exercised against himself. "A house divided against itself cannot stand." It is evident that it is the Spirit of God who hinders Satan's man and Satan's projects until the divinely appointed time. There is no hint that Satan will withdraw, or be removed out of the way before this "man of sin" can be revealed; but there is a sense in which the Spirit will be removed. That particular relationship or Presence which began with the Church and has continued with the Church will naturally cease when the Church is removed. As the Omnipresent One, the Spirit will remain, but His present ministry and abode in the Church will have been changed. The Spirit was in the world before Pentecost; yet we are told that He came on that day as had been promised. He came in the sense that He took up a new abode in the Church — the body of believers — and a new ministry in the world. This ministry will cease when the Church is gathered out and His abode will be ended when His temple of living stones is removed. Thus it may be concluded that His going will be but the reversal of Pentecost and will not imply His entire absence from the world. He will rather return to those relationships and ministries which were His before this dispensation began. There are clear assurances of the presence and power of the Spirit in the world after the departure of the Church. The restraining power of the Spirit will be withdrawn and the Church removed at a time known to God, and then will the forces of darkness be permitted to come to their final display and judgment.

An evidence of the Spirit's power to restrain may be seen in the fact that with all their profanity men do not now swear in the name of the Holy Spirit. There is a restraining power in the world and it is evidently one of the present ministries of the Spirit.

Second, The Ministry of the Spirit in Reproving the World of Sin, Righteousness and Judgment.

This ministry, by its very nature, must be a dealing with the individual, rather than with the world as a whole. The passage reads: "And when he is come, he will reprove the world of sin, and of righteousness, and of judgment: of sin, because they believe not on me; of righteousness, because I go to my Father, and ye see me no more; of judgment, because the prince of this world is judged" (John 16:8-11). This passage indicates a three-fold ministry.

(1) The Spirit enlightens the unsaved with regard to *one* sin only: "Of sin, because they believe not on me." The full judg-

ment of sin has been taken up and completed at the cross (John 1:29). Hence a lost man must be made aware of the fact that, because of the cross, his present obligation to God is that of *accepting* God's provided cure for his sins. In this ministry, the Spirit does not shame the unsaved because of their sins; but He reveals the fact of a Saviour, and One who may be received or rejected.

(2) The Spirit illuminates the unsaved with respect to right- eousness and that "because I go to my Father, and ye see me no more." How can a sinner be made righteous in the eyes of a Holy God? It will not be by any attempted self-improvement. There is a righteousness for him *from* God, which is *unto* all and *upon* all who *believe*. It is foreign to the wisdom of this world that a perfect righteousness can be gained by simply *believing*, and believing on an invisible Person who is at the right hand of God; yet every lost soul must, in some measure, sense this great possibility if he is to be constrained to turn to Christ from self.

(3) So, also, the Spirit, in this three-fold ministry, illuminates the unsaved concerning a divine judgment which is already past; for "the prince of this world is judged." By this illumination the unsaved are made to realize that it is not a problem of getting God to be merciful in His judgments of their sins: they are rather to *believe* that the judgment is wholly past and that they have only to rest in the priceless victory that is won. Every claim of Satan over man because of sin has been broken, and so per- fectly that God, who is infinitely holy, can now receive and save sinners. Principalities and powers were triumphed over in the cross (Colossians 2:13-15).

Undoubtedly it is the purpose of God that the Spirit shall use such instrumentalities as He may choose in illuminating the world with respect to sin, righteousness, and judgment. He may use a preacher, a portion of the Scriptures, a Christian's testimony, or a printed message; but back of all this is the effective opera- tion of the Spirit.

Thus the Spirit ministers to the world, actualizing to them otherwise unknowable facts which, taken together, form the central truths of the Gospel of His grace.

Third, The Ministry of the Spirit in Regenerating.

This and the three following ministries of the Spirit enter into the salvation of the one who believes on Christ. He is born of the Spirit (John 3:6) and has become a legitimate child of God. He has "partaken of the divine nature" and Christ is begotten in him "the hope of glory." As he is a child of God, he is also an "heir of God, and a joint-heir with Jesus Christ." The new divine nature is more deeply implanted in his being than the human nature of his earthly father or mother. This transformation is accomplished when he *believes,* and is never repeated; for the Bible knows nothing of a second regeneration by the Spirit.

Fourth, The Ministry of the Spirit as Indwelling the Believer.

The fact that the Spirit now indwells every believer is one of the outstanding characteristics of this age. It is one of the most vital contrasts between law and grace.[1]

It is divinely purposed that under grace the believer's life is to be lived in the unbroken power of the Spirit. The Christian has but to contemplate his utter helplessness, or consider carefully the emphasis given to this truth in the New Testament to become aware of the greatness of the gift which provides the indwelling Spirit. This gift was considered by the early Christians to be the fundamental fact of the believer's new estate. We read in the account of the first preaching of the Gospel to the Jews at Pentecost that the gift of the Spirit was the new fact of surpassing importance. In this same period of Jewish preaching as recorded in Acts 5:32 the Spirit is said to be given to all who obey the Gospel invitation and command. So, also, the transcendent fact of the gift is emphasized in the records of the first preaching of the Gospel to the Gentiles. Pentecost could not be repeated; but there was a very special demonstration of the Spirit in connection with this preaching. This demonstration was evidently given in order to provide against any conclusions to the effect that the Spirit was not given as fully

---

[1]See also page 65.

to Gentiles as to Jews. We read: "While Peter yet spake these words, the Holy Ghost fell on all them which heard the word. And they of the circumcision which believed were astonished, as many as came with Peter, because that on the Gentiles also was poured out the gift of the Holy Ghost. For they heard them speak with tongues, and magnify God. Then answered Peter, can any man forbid water, that these should not be baptized, which have received the Holy Ghost as well as we?" (Acts 10:44-47). In connection with Peter's explanation to the Jewish believers of his ministry to the Gentiles, we read: "And as I began to speak, the Holy Ghost fell on them, as at the beginning. Then remembered I the word of the Lord, how that he said, John indeed baptized with water; but ye shall be baptized with the Holy Ghost. Forasmuch then as God gave them the like gift as he did unto us, who believed on the Lord Jesus Christ; what was I, that I could withstand God?" (Acts 11:15-17). Though there are other issues connected with the filling of the Spirit for power, it is evident that the gift of the Spirit is God's priceless gift to every one who has been saved. The Biblical importance placed upon this gift far exceeds the importance which Christians usually place upon it.

The *fact* of the indwelling Spirit is not revealed through any experience whatsoever; nevertheless that fact is the foundation upon which all other ministries to the child of God must depend. It is impossible for one to enter into the plan and provision for a life of power and blessing and ignore the distinct revelation as to *where* the Spirit is now as related to the believer. It must be understood and fully believed that the Spirit is now *indwelling* the true child of God and that He indwells from the moment the believer is saved. (1) The Bible explicitly teaches this, and (2) reason demands it in the light of other revelations:

(a) *According to Revelation*

The fact that the Spirit indwells the believer is now to be considered without reference to the other ministries of the Spirit. Any ministry of the Spirit taken alone would be incomplete; but it is of particular importance that the Spirit's ministry of indwelling be seen by itself. A few passages of Scripture may suffice to indicate the Bible teaching on this important theme.

John 7:37-39, "In the last day, that great day of the feast, Jesus stood and cried, saying, If any man thirst, let him come unto me, and drink. He that believeth on me, as the scripture hath said, out of his belly [inner life] shall flow rivers of living water. (But this spake he of the Spirit, which they that believe on him should receive: for the Holy Spirit was not yet given; because Jesus was not yet glorified.)" This passage contains the distinct promise that *all* in this dispensation who believe on Him receive the Spirit *when* they believe.

Acts 11:17, "Forasmuch then as God gave them the like gift as he did unto us, who believed on the Lord Jesus Christ; what was I, that I could withstand God?" This is Peter's account of the first preaching of the Gospel to the Gentiles. He states that the Gentiles received the Spirit when they *believed* as the Jews had done. The one condition was believing on Christ for salvation and the Spirit was received as a vital part of that salvation.

Romans 5:5, "Because the love of God is shed abroad in our hearts by the Spirit which is given unto us."

Romans 8:9, "But ye are not in the flesh, but in the Spirit, if so be that the Spirit of God dwell in you. Now if any man have not the Spirit of Christ, he is none of his." This is a clear reference to the *indwelling* Spirit. Not only is the very fact of salvation to be tested by His presence; but every quickening of the "mortal body" depends on "His Spirit that dwelleth in you" (v. 11).

Romans 8:23, "And not only they [all creation], but ourselves also, which have the firstfruits of the Spirit." There is no reference here to some class of Christians. *All* Christians have the "firstfruits of the Spirit."

I Corinthians 2:12, "Now we have received . . . the Spirit which is of God." Again the reference is not to a class of believers: *all* have received the Spirit.

I Corinthians 6:19, 20, "What? know ye not that your body is the temple of the Holy Spirit which is in you, which ye have of God, and ye are not your own? For ye are bought with a price:

therefore glorify God in your body, and in your spirit, which are God's." This, again, is not a reference to some class of very holy Christians. The context reveals them to be guilty of most serious sin, and the fact of the indwelling Spirit is made the basis of this appeal. They are not told that unless they cease from sin they will lose the Spirit. They are told that they *have* the Spirit in them and are appealed to on this sole ground to turn to a life of holiness and purity. There were much deeper realities for these sinning Christians in their relation to the Spirit; but *receiving* the Spirit was not their problem. He was already indwelling them.

I Corinthians 12:13, "And have been all made to drink into one Spirit." The same very faulty Corinthian Christians are included in the word *"all"* (see also, v. 7).

II Corinthians 5:5, "God, who also hath given unto us the earnest of the Spirit." Again, it is not *some* Christians, but *all*.

Galatians 3:2, "This only would I learn of you, Received ye the Spirit by the works of the law, or by the hearing of faith?" It was by faith and the Spirit has been received by *all* who have exercised saving faith.

Galatians 4:6, "And because ye are sons [not because ye are sanctified], God hath sent forth the Spirit of his Son into your hearts, crying, Abba, Father."

I John 3:23, "And hereby we know that he abideth in us, by the Spirit which he hath given unto us."

I John 4:13, "Hereby know we that we dwell in him, and he in us, because he hath given us of his Spirit."

The indwelling Spirit is an "unction" and an "anointing" for *each* child of God; for these words are not used concerning a *class* of believers (I John 2:20, 27).

There are three passages which have seemed to some to confuse the clear teaching of the Scriptures just given and these should be considered.

(1) Acts 5:32, "And we are his witnesses of these things; and so is also the Holy Spirit, whom God hath given to them that obey him." This is not the daily life obedience of a Chris-

tian. It is an appeal to unsaved men for "the obedience of faith." The passage teaches that the Spirit is given to those who obey God concerning faith in His Son as Saviour. The context is clear.

(2) Acts 8:14-17, has already been considered. It falls within the brief period between Pentecost and the preaching of the Gospel to the Gentiles. The conditions existing at that time should not be taken as the final relationship between the Spirit and all believers throughout this age.

(3) Acts 19:1-6, "And it came to pass, that, while Apollos was at Corinth, Paul having passed through the upper coasts came to Ephesus: and finding certain disciples [not necessarily Christians], he said unto them, Have ye received the Holy Spirit since ye believed [or, did ye receive the Holy Spirit *when* ye believed? See all versions]? And they said unto him, We have not so much as heard whether there be any Holy Spirit. And he said unto them, Unto what then were ye baptized? and they said, Unto John's baptism. Then said Paul, John verily baptized with the baptism of repentance, saying unto the people, that they should believe on him which should come after him, that is, on Christ Jesus. When they heard this, they were baptized in the name of the Lord Jesus." These "disciples" were disciples, or proselytes, of John the Baptist. They knew little of Christ, or of the way of salvation by believing, or of the Holy Spirit. Paul had immediately missed the evidence of the presence of the Spirit in these disciples and so struck at the vital point with the question, "Upon believing did ye receive the Spirit?" After they heard of salvation through Christ, and believed, the Apostle is said to have "laid his hands upon them," and "the Holy Spirit came on them; and they spake with tongues and prophesied." The laying on of hands, like the signs which followed, is Biblically related to the Spirit as being *upon* them, or *filling* them; but should not be confused with the fact that they had received the Spirit when they believed.

There is, therefore, no Scripture which contradicts the clear testimony of the Bible that *all* believers of this dispensation have the Spirit in them.

(b) *According to Reason*

A holy life and walk, which must always depend on the enabling power of the Spirit, is as much demanded of one believer as of another. There is not one standard of life for one class of believers, and another standard of life for another class of believers. If there is a child of God who has not the Spirit in him, he must, with all reason, be excused from those responsibilities which anticipate the power and presence of the Spirit. The fact that God addresses all believers as though they possess the Spirit is sufficient evidence that they *have* the Spirit.

It may be concluded, then, that all believers *have* the Spirit. This does not imply that they have entered into all the possible blessings of a Spirit-filled life. They have the Spirit when they are saved and there is no record that He ever withdraws. His is an *abiding* presence.

Fifth, The Ministry of the Spirit in Baptizing.

Reference has already been made to this particular ministry of the Spirit as related to the Day of Pentecost. The full Bible teaching of this theme is presented in a very few passages (Matthew 3:11; Mark 1:8; Luke 3:16; John 1:33; Acts 1:5; 11:16; Romans 6:3-4; I Corinthians 12:13; Galatians 3:27; Ephesians 4:5; Colossians 2:12). Of these passages, only one unfolds the meaning: "For by one Spirit are we all baptized into one body, whether we be Jews or Gentiles, whether we be bond or free; and have been all made to drink into one Spirit" (I Corinthians 12:13, cf. Romans 6:3). In no Scripture is this ministry of the Spirit directly related to power or service. It has to do with the forming of the body of Christ out of living members, and when one is united vitally and organically to Christ, he has been "baptized into one body," and has been "made to drink into one Spirit" (cf. v. 12). Being a member in the body of Christ, anticipates service; but service is always related to another ministry than the baptism of the Spirit. Since the baptism with the Spirit is the organic placing of the believer into Christ, it is that operation of God which establishes every position and standing

of the Christian. No other divine undertaking in salvation is so
far reaching in its effect. It is because of this new union to
Christ that a Christian can be said to be "in Christ," and being
"in Christ" he partakes of *all* that Christ is, — His life, His righteousness, and His glory. The unbeliever, who is "without Christ,"
enters completely into this union with Christ the moment he
believes.[1]

The organic relationship to the body of Christ is accomplished
as a part of the great divine undertaking in salvation which is
performed when saving faith is exercised. There is no indication
that this baptizing ministry of the Spirit would be undertaken
a second time. A possible distinction as to whether the baptism of the Spirit was accomplished at Pentecost *provisionally* for
all who accept Christ in this dispensation, or whether it is
individual when they believe is of no moment in this discussion.
It is important to discover the exact meaning of the word as
representing a particular ministry of the Spirit.

Sixth, The Ministry of the Spirit in Sealing.

"And grieve not the Holy Spirit of God whereby ye are sealed
unto the day of redemption" (Ephesians 4:30, See also, II
Corinthians 1:22; Ephesians 1:13). The ministry of the Spirit
in sealing evidently represents the Godward aspect of the relationship, — authority, responsibility, and a final transaction. It is

---

[1]In two synoptic Gospels the promise of the baptism with the Spirit is
accompanied with a promise of a baptism with fire (Matthew 3:11;
Luke 3:16). Just what is meant by a baptism with fire has been the
subject of much discussion. "Cloven tongues like as of fire" sat on a
few on the Day of Pentecost; but this has not been the experience of
all believers. The judgment of the believer's works at the judgment
seat of Christ (I Corinthians 3:9-15; II Corinthians 5:10) is the only
contact with fire which is determined for *all* who are saved. It is
therefore probable that this judgment is the baptism with fire. There
is a deep correspondence between the baptism with the Spirit and
this baptism with fire. As the baptism with the Spirit provides the
saved one with a perfect standing for time and eternity, so the baptism
with fire will provide the saved one with a perfect state which will fit
him for heaven itself. At the judgment seat of Christ, His eyes of
fire (Revelation 1:14) will burn away all the dross and only that
which is heavenly will abide.

"unto the day of redemption." The Spirit Himself is the seal, and *all* who have the Spirit are sealed. His presence in the heart is the divine mark. This ministry of the Spirit is also performed when faith is exercised for salvation, and this ministry could not be repeated since the first sealing of any believer is "unto the day of redemption."

There are, then, four ministries of the Spirit for the believer which are wrought at the moment he is saved and are never accomplished a second time. He is said to be born, indwelt (or anointed), baptized, and sealed of the Spirit. It may also be added that these four operations of the Spirit *in* and *for* the child of God are not related to an *experience*. The Spirit may actualize all this to the believer after he is saved, and it may then become the occasion for most blessed joy and consolation. These four general ministries which are performed *in* and *for* believers alike constitute the "Earnest of the Spirit" (II Corinthians 1:22; 5:5), and the "Firstfruits of the Spirit" (Romans 8:23).

Seventh, The Ministry of the Spirit in Filling.

The fact, extent and conditions of this ministry of the Spirit constitute the message of this book and will occupy the following chapters. What has gone before has been written that the filling of the Spirit might not be confused with any other of His operations.

CHAPTER 3

THE FILLING OF THE SPIRIT, OR TRUE SPIRITUALITY

BY VARIOUS TERMS the Bible teaches that there are two classes of Christians: those who "abide in Christ," and those who "abide not"; those who are "walking in the light," and those who "walk in darkness"; those who "walk by the Spirit," and those who "walk as men"; those who "walk in newness of life," and those who "walk after the flesh"; those who have the Spirit *"in"* and *"upon"* them, and those who have the Spirit *"in"* them, but not *"upon"* them; those who are "spiritual" and those who are "carnal"; those who are "filled with the Spirit," and those who are not. All this has to do with the quality of daily life of saved people, and is in no way a contrast between the saved and the unsaved. Where there is such an emphasis in the Bible as is indicated by these distinctions there is a corresponding reality. There is, then, the possibility of a great transition for those who are carnal into the reality of true spiritual living. The revelation concerning this possible transition, with all of its experiences and blessings, is taken seriously only by earnest believers who are faithfully seeking a God-honoring daily life. To such there is boundless joy and consolation in this gospel of deliverance, power and victory.

The transition from the carnal to the spiritual, is treated at length in the Bible. However, it is possible to know the doctrine and not to have entered into its blessings; as it is possible, on the other hand, to have entered in some measure into the experience and not to have known the doctrine. This gospel of deliverance has suffered much from those who have sought to understand its principles by analyzing some personal experience apart from the teaching of the Scriptures. The danger in this error is obvious: No one experience would ever be a true, or complete representa-

40

tion of the full purpose of God for every Christian; and if it were, nothing short of the infinite wisdom of God could formulate its exact statement. For want of Bible instruction many, when attempting to account for an experience, have coined terms and phrases which are not Biblical and are therefore invariably as faulty as any of the conclusions of the finite mind when attempting to deal with the divine realities. It would be useless to attempt to classify experiences; but when one has found peace, power and blessing through a definite yielding to God and reliance on His strength alone, the Bible clearly assigns the cause to be a larger manifestation of the presence and power of the Spirit. Such an one is "filled with the Spirit."

WHAT IS THE SPIRIT'S FILLING?

In the Bible, the meaning of the phrase "filled with the Spirit," is disclosed, and the filling of the Spirit is also seen to be the experience of the early Christians. From the Word of God, then, we can hope to arrive at some clear understanding of what is meant by the phrase, the "filling of the Spirit"; but there is no instruction to be gained from such man-made, unbiblical terms as "second blessing," "a second work of grace," "the higher life," and various phrases used in the perverted statements of the doctrines of sanctification and perfection. An unlimited field lies before us when we are told that we may be "changed from glory to glory" even into the image of Christ, and that by the Spirit (II Corinthians 3:18). What this transformation may mean to a believer and the exact conditions upon which it may be realized, must be understood, not from the imperfect analysis of experience, but from the exact words of revelation. It is quite possible for any child of God to make full proof of 'that good, and acceptable, and perfect will of God" for him. And God has promised to work in the believer "both to will and to do of his good pleasure." By His power the very "virtues of him who called us out of darkness into his marvellous light" and the "mind of Christ" may be reproduced in the one who is saved. These blessings and the conditions God imposes for their attainment are clearly set forth in the Word of God.

The Spirit does not speak from Himself. His purpose is to reveal and glorify Christ (John 16:12-15). The Spirit is made known to us by descriptive titles, such as "The Holy Spirit," or "The Spirit of God"; but His name is not disclosed. Though He does not reveal Himself, He is, nevertheless, the *cause* of all true spirituality. His work is to manifest "the life that is Christ" so completely that one can say: "For to me to live is Christ"; but the sufficient power back of this possible out-living of Christ is the in-living Spirit of God, and this is a result of the Spirit's filling.

Paul had been saved on the Damascus road and there, we may believe, had received the Spirit as the "earnest" and the "first-fruits." Later, after having entered into the city, Ananias came to him and placing his hands on him said, "Brother Saul, the Lord, even Jesus, that appeared unto thee in the way as thou camest, hath sent me, that thou mightest receive thy sight, and be filled with the Holy Spirit." Two results were to be accomplished: Saul was to receive his sight, and he was to be filled with the Spirit, This, it should be remembered, was no part of his salvation. We are then told that "immediately there fell from his eyes as it had been scales: and he received sight forthwith." There is no record of an emotion, or experience, which might be taken as evidence that he had been filled with the Spirit. He was filled, nevertheless, as definitely as he regained his sight. The evidence is conclusive; for the record goes on to say: "and straightway he preached Christ in the synagogues, that he is the Son of God" (Acts 9:17-20). There is no evidence that the Apostle was conscious of the Spirit; he was altogether occupied with Christ. Nevertheless, he was "filled with the Spirit" and so, in the Spirit's own time and way, entered into the priceless result of an out-lived Christ. The Spirit is the *cause* while the experience of the glory and reality of Christ is the *effect*.

According to the Scriptures, the Spirit-filled believer is the divine ideal, whether it be by example, or precept.

First, as to example: Christ was "full of the Spirit" (Luke 4:1); each of the members of one family, Zacharias, Elisabeth and John, were "filled with the Spirit" (Luke 1:15, 41, 67); and the disciples and others were filled again and again after their real ministry had begun (Acts 2:4; 4:8, 31; 6:3; 7:55; 9:17; 11:24; 13:52. Note, also, all passages where the Spirit is said to have been "*upon*" believers).

Second, as to precept: One direct New Testament command is given: "And be not drunk with wine, wherein is excess; but be filled with the Spirit" (or, more literally, "be being kept filled by the Spirit." Ephesians 5:18). Here the form of the verb used is somewhat different from that which is used in connection with the other ministries of the Spirit. The Christian *has been* born, baptized, indwelt, and sealed by the Spirit: he must *be getting* (being kept) filled by the Spirit. It is the revealed purpose of God that the Spirit shall be constantly ministered unto the Christian: "He therefore that ministereth to you the Spirit" (Galatians 3:5). A Christian, to be spiritual, must, then, be filled and kept filled by the Spirit. An experience may or may not accompany the first entrance into the Spirit-filled life; but, even when there is an experience, the Bible knows nothing of a "second blessing," or "second work of grace," wherein there will be any less need of the mighty enabling power of God tomorrow than there has been today. One may learn better *how* to "walk in the Spirit"; but he will never come to a moment in this life when he will need to walk *less* by the Spirit. The divine resources for a moment by moment triumph in Christ are limitless; but the utter need of the helpless creature never ceases.

It is important to note that three times in the New Testament the effect of strong drink is put over against the Spirit-filled life (Luke 1:15; Acts 2:12-21; Ephesians 5:18). As strong drink stimulates the physical forces and men are prone to turn to it for help over the difficult places, so the child of God, facing an impossible responsibility of a heavenly walk and service, is directed to the Spirit as the source of all sufficiency. Every moment in a spiritual life is one of unmeasured need and superhuman demands, and the supply of enabling power and grace must be as constantly received and employed. "As thy day, so shall thy strength be."

To be filled with the Spirit is to have the Spirit fulfilling in us all that God intended Him to do when He placed Him there. To be filled is not the problem of getting *more* of the Spirit: it is rather the problem of the Spirit getting *more* of us. We shall never have *more* of the Spirit than the anointing which every true Christian has received. On the other hand, the Spirit may have all of the believer and thus be able to manifest in him the life and character of Christ. A spiritual person, then, is one who experiences the divine purpose and plan in his daily life through the power of the indwelling Spirit. The *character* of that life will be the out-lived Christ. The *cause* of that life will be the unhindered indwelling Spirit (Ephesians 3:16-21; II Corinthians 3:18).

The New Testament is clear as to just what the Spirit would produce in a fully adjusted life, and all of this revelation taken together forms the Bible definition of spirituality. These undertakings are distinctly assigned to the Spirit, and are His manifestations in and through the Christian.

SEVEN MANIFESTATIONS OF THE SPIRIT

There are seven manifestations of the Spirit, and these are said to be experienced only by the Spirit-filled believer; for in the Scriptures, these results are never related to any other ministry of the Spirit than that of *filling*. The seven manifestations of the Spirit are:

I. THE SPIRIT PRODUCES CHRISTIAN CHARACTER

"But the fruit of the Spirit is love, joy, peace, longsuffering, gentleness, goodness, faith, meekness, temperance" (self-control, Galatians 5:22, 23).

Compressed into these nine words we have not only the exact statement as to what Christian character is, but a description, as well, of the life that Christ lived while here on the earth. It is also a statement of that manner of life which He would have the Christian experience here and now. These nine words form a Bible definition of what is meant by the phrase, "For to me to live is Christ." Though the world strives at a shadow of what these nine words represent, the reality is foreign to human nature, even when that nature is at its best. These graces, as here presented, are exotics and are never found in human nature unless produced there by the power of God. They are the "fruit of the Spirit." Christian character, therefore, is not developed, or "built" through human attention and energy. The method of attaining unto a character by attention and energy, which is now elaborately explained and constantly recommended by many, is the best the world can do, and that method may have some realization within the sphere of the shadows the world has chosen as its ideals. The child of God is not facing the mere shadows which are the ideals of the world, though in ignorance he might suppose that he is. He is facing the problem of shewing "forth the praises [virtues] of him" who hath called us "out of darkness into his marvellous light." He will find little encouragement in the Bible to attempt the *"building"* of these characteristics of the Infinite. Human nature in its most favorable conditions has never been expected to do this. If the aim were no higher than the standards of the world, it might seem reasonable to try to build a Christian character; but even then, there would be no Scripture to warrant the human struggle. True Christian character is the *"fruit of the Spirit."*

The very position of a child of God as a heavenly citizen demands that these nine graces which are the "fruit of the Spirit" shall be present in his daily life. He is to "walk worthy" of the calling wherewith he is called, "with all lowliness and meekness, with longsuffering, forbearing one another in love." So, also, on the other hand, his priceless fellowship "with the Father and with his Son" must depend on the presence of these divine characteristics. There must be some quality of life and character in the Christian with which God can have fellowship. But if God finds anything like Himself in a human life, He must place it there; for He knows full well that such divine graces can never appear in a life apart from His own power. Thus if He, by His very nature, demands the heavenly graces as the only possible basis for communion with His Spirit-born child, He is not unreasonable in such a demand, for He does not expect these graces from the flesh, but has made full provision that they may be produced by the Spirit. The fact, however, that He has *designed* that they shall be the "fruit of the Spirit" changes the whole human responsibility. It is no longer something for the human strength to attempt, nor is it to be done by the human strength plus the help of the Spirit. It is not something that man can do, even with help. It is *"the fruit of the Spirit."* True Christian character is produced *in* the believer, but not *by* the believer. Doubtless the Spirit employs every faculty of the believer's being to realize this priceless quality of life; yet there is nothing in the believer, of himself, which could produce this result. There is not even a spark of these graces within the human nature which might be fanned into a fire. *All* must be produced in the heart and life by the Spirit. Thus the new problem is naturally that of maintaining such a relationship to the Spirit as shall make it possible for Him to accomplish *continually* what He came into the heart to do.

What the flesh *can, will* and *must* do has been stated in the preceding verses of the passage under consideration: "Now the works of the flesh are manifest, which are these; Adultery, fornication, uncleanness, lasciviousness, idolatry, witchcraft, hatred, variance, emulations, wrath, strife, seditions; heresies, envyings, murders, drunkenness, revellings, and such like." "But," in contrast to all this, "the fruit of the Spirit is love, joy, peace, long-suffering, gentleness, goodness, faith, meekness, temperance" (self-control). "The flesh," according to its use in this and similar passages is more than the physical body. The term represents *all*, — spirit, soul and body — that the person was before he was saved. From that source there can come no real spiritual "fruit." In this very context it is stated that "the flesh lusteth against the Spirit, and the Spirit against the flesh: and these are contrary the one to the other."[1]

There are, then, two principles of life which are open to the child of God: the carnal walk which is by the energy of the flesh, or "as men," and the spiritual walk which is by the energy of the Spirit, or as Christ. This passage in Galatians states:

[1]See also page 113.

"This I say then, Walk in the Spirit [lit. by means of the Spirit], and ye shall not fulfil the lust [desire] of the flesh." These two principles are absolutely opposed to each other and therefore cannot be mingled. Walking by means of the Spirit, or "being led of the Spirit," is not the flesh being *helped* in some degree by the Spirit. It is said to be a direct accomplishment of the Spirit in spite of the *opposition* of the flesh.

When walking by the Spirit the results are celestial: "Ye shall not fulfil the lust of the flesh"; "So that ye cannot [when walking by the Spirit] do the things that ye [otherwise] would"; "If ye are led of the Spirit ye are not under the law"; and "The fruit of the Spirit is love, joy, peace, longsuffering, gentleness, goodness, faith, meekness, temperance" (self-control).

Such results are priceless. The world looks on to the end of a long process of self-training and self-repression for the realization of the human virtues the sum of which is called "character." The Christian may realize *at once* the heavenly virtues of Christ: not by trying; but by a right adjustment to the indwelling Spirit. This is a *revelation*, quite foreign indeed to man's habits of thinking and acting, and it is to many a "hard saying." This tremendous possibility, as revealed from God, will not seem reasonable to one who is not yet done with doubt as to the possibility of the supernatural being experienced in every moment of life. Such doubters should not contend that, because to them unreal, the walk by means of the Spirit is not God's gracious provision for His children. The revelation that true Christian character is directly produced as a fruit of the indwelling Spirit stands on the pages of God's Word. Clear statements are made and the Bible teaching on this subject is direct and uncomplicated. Not only so, but there are many who are joyous witnesses that it is a reality in their personal experience.

The effects of Christian growth are not included in this immediate victory. It is simply the result of entering into the whole of the present will of God for our lives.

The nine words which define Christian character may be traced through the New Testament and, when so traced, it will be found (1) that they are always presented as being *divine* characteristics, though they sometimes have a shadow of their reality in the relationships and ideals of the world; (2) they are assuredly *expected* by God in the believer's life; and (3) they are always *produced* only by the Spirit of God. Each of these nine words might profitably be considered at length; but space can be given to one only. What is found to be true of the one word may measure, to some extent, what would be found to be true of all these words.

LOVE

There is a very real human love; but all Christian love, according to the Scriptures, is distinctly a manifestation of divine love *through* the human heart. A statement of this is found in Romans 5:5, "because the love of God is shed abroad [lit. gushes forth] in our hearts by [produced, or caused by] the Holy Spirit, which is given unto us." This is not the working of the human affection; it is rather the direct manifestation of the "love of God" passing *through* the heart of the believer *out from* the indwelling Spirit. It is the realization of the last petition of the High Priestly prayer of our Lord: "That the love wherewith thou hast loved me may be in them" (John 17:26). It is simply God's love working *in* and *through* the believer. It could not be humanly produced, or even successfully imitated and it, of necessity, goes out to the objects of divine affection and grace, rather than to the objects of human desire. A human heart cannot *produce* divine love, but it can *experience* it. To have a heart that feels the compassion of God is to drink of the wine of heaven. In considering this imparted love of God it should be noted:

First, The love of God imparted is not experienced by the unsaved: "But I know you, that ye have not the love of God in you" (John 5:42).

Second, The love of God reaches out for the whole world: "For God so loved the world" (John 3:16); "That he by the grace of God should taste death for every man" (Hebrews 2:9); "And he is the propitiation for our sins; and not for ours only, but also for the sins of the whole world" (I John 2:2). This is a divine love for the world of lost men. It is God's affection which knows no bounds. What is sometimes called "the missionary spirit" is none other than that compassion, which brought the Son of God from heaven, "gushing forth" *through* a human heart. Interest in lost men is not secured by an attempted development of human affections: it is immediately realized in a Christian heart when there is a right relation to the Spirit of God. A desire for the salvation of others is the first thought of many after they are born again.

Third, The love of God abhors the present world system. "Love not the world, neither the things that are in the world. If any man love the world, the love of the Father is not in him. For all that is in the world, the lust of the flesh, the lust of the eyes, and the pride of life, is not of the Father, but is of the world" (I John 2:15, 16). Such purified love will always be the experience of the one in whom the love of God is imparted.

Fourth, The love of God is toward His Spirit-born children. "Much more then, being now justified by his blood, we shall be saved from wrath through him. For if, when we were enemies, we were reconciled to God by the death of his Son, much more, being reconciled, we shall be saved by his life" (Romans 5:9, 10); "Christ also loved the church, and gave himself for it" (Ephesians 5:25). He loves His own even though they are wandering away, as is revealed in the return of the "prodigal son." "If we love one another, God dwelleth in us, and His love is perfected in us" (I John 4:12). By this divine compassion the Christian proves his reality before the world: "A new commandment I give unto you, That ye love one another; as I have loved you, that ye also love one another. By this shall all men know that ye are my disciples, if ye have love one to another" (John 13:34, 35). Such divine love is also the test of our brotherhood in Christ: "Hereby perceive we the love of God, because he laid down his life for us: and we ought to lay down our lives for the brethren. But whoso hath this world's good, and seeth his brother have need, and shutteth up his bowels of compassion from him, how dwelleth the love of God in him?" (I John 3:16, 17); "We know we have passed from death unto life, because we love the brethren" (I John 3:14).

Fifth, The love of God is without end: "Having loved his own which were in the world, he loved them unto the end" (eternally, John 13:1). The love of God in the believer is said to "suffer long" and then is *kind*.

Sixth, The love of God is toward Israel: "Yea, I have loved thee with an everlasting love" (Jeremiah 31:3). So the Spirit-filled believer will learn to rejoice in the great prophecies and purposes of God for that people with whom He is in everlasting covenants, and for whom He has an everlasting love.

Seventh, The love of God is sacrificial: "For ye know the grace of our Lord Jesus Christ, that, though he was rich, yet for your sakes he became poor, that ye through his poverty might be rich" (II Corinthians 8:9). Such an attitude on the part of the Son of God toward the eternal riches must, if reproduced in the Christian, affect largely his attitude toward earthly riches.

Not only is the love of God sacrificial as to heavenly riches; it is sacrificial as to life itself. "Hereby perceive we the love of God, because he laid down his life for us." It therefore follows: "And we ought to lay down our lives for the brethren" (I John 3:16, 17). The Apostle Paul testified: "I say the truth in Christ, I lie not, my conscience also bearing me witness in the Holy Spirit, that I have great heaviness and continual sorrow in my heart. For I could wish that myself were accursed from Christ for my brethren, my kinsmen according to the flesh" (Romans 9:1-3). The Apostle knew full well that there was no occasion for him to be accursed since his Lord had been made a curse for all; but he could still be *willing* to be made a curse. Such an experience is the direct outworking in a human life of the divine love which gave Jesus to die under the curse and judgments of the sin of the world. When this divine compassion for lost men is reproduced in the believer, it becomes the true and sufficient dynamic for soul-saving work.

Thus the mighty heart of God may be manifested in a human life, and this one word "love," together with the other eight words which indicate the fruit of the Spirit, is a representation of true Christian character. The other eight words, when traced in the Scriptures, will also prove to be divine graces which are realized in the human heart only as they are *imparted*. "My joy shall be in you." "My peace I give unto you."

These divine graces are not produced in every Christian's heart. They are produced in those who are "by the Spirit walking."

II. THE SPIRIT PRODUCES CHRISTIAN SERVICE

Here again, turning from human reason to Bible doctrine, we discover Christian service to be a direct exercise of the energy of the Spirit through the believer. "From within him shall flow rivers of living water. But this spake he of the Spirit" (John 7:38, 39, R. V.). Human energy could never produce "living waters," and certainly not in "*rivers*." This statement is keyed to the Infinite. The human, at best, could be no more than the channel, or instrument, for the divine outflow.

The very service of the Christian, like his salvation, has been designed in the eternal plan and purpose of God: "For we are his workmanship, created in Christ Jesus unto good works, which God hath before ordained that we should walk in them" (Ephesians 2:10). According to this passage, God hath before ordained a very special service for each individual to perform, and the doing of these particular and individual ministries constitutes "good works" according to the divine estimates. Any service other than that which was foreordained for the individual, though valuable in itself, cannot be called "good works" because it is not the personal outworking of the will of God. The discovery and realization of "good works" is not experienced by all believers, but only by those who have presented their bodies a living sacrifice, holy, acceptable unto God; who are not "conformed to this world," but are "transformed" (transfigured) by the renewing of their minds (Romans 12:1, 2).

Christian service, according to the New Testament, is the exercise of a "gift." The Bible use of the word "gift" should not be confused with the world's conception of a "gifted person." The thought of the world concerning a gifted person is of one who by physical birth, is especially able to accomplish certain things. Such natural ability the Spirit will doubtless employ; but a "gift," in the Bible use of the word, is a direct undertaking, or manifestation, of the Spirit working *through* the believer. It is the Spirit of God doing something, and using the believer to accomplish it; rather than the believer doing something, and calling on God for help in the task. It is the "work of the Lord" in which we are to "*abound*." According to the Word, the Spirit produces Christian service as He produces the graces of Christ *in* and *through* the believer. Every faculty of the human instrument will be employed in the work. That human instrument will know what it is to be weary and worn in the service. Human energy, however, could never produce the divine results which are anticipated, and the Scriptures jealously contend that true Christian service is a direct "manifestation of the Spirit": "Now there are diversities of gifts, but the same Spirit." Though no two Christians are doing the same service, the Spirit produces the energy and accomplishes the individual and particular work in each. "And there are differences of administrations, but the same Lord. And there are diversities of operations, but it is the same God which worketh [energizes] all in all. But the manifestation of the Spirit is given to every [Christian] man to profit withal. For to one is given by the Spirit the word of wisdom; to another the word of knowledge by the same Spirit; to another faith by the same Spirit; to another the gifts of healing by the same Spirit; to another the working of miracles; to another prophecy; to another discerning of spirits; to another divers kinds of tongues; to another the interpretation of tongues: but all these worketh [are wrought by] that one and the selfsame Spirit, dividing to every man severally as he will" (I Corinthians 12:4-11).

A "gift," then, is a "manifestation of the Spirit," or service divinely produced by the Spirit, and "as he will." Thus it is clear that there can be no exercise of a gift through an unyielded life.

It is probable that the "gifts" enumerated in the Bible were the outstanding manifestations of the Spirit according to the conditions and time when the record was written. Some have proved abiding to the present hour. Other manifestations of the Spirit have evidently ceased. This is not due to failing piety after the first generation of Christians. There is no evidence of a decrease of piety. Those manifestations of the Spirit which have ceased were doubtless related to the *introduction* rather than the *continuation* of the work of the Spirit in this age. This is not without precedent: When Christ was born, a star was seen in the East, the voices of the angelic host were heard and most unusual conditions obtained. The star did not continue to shine. The angel voices were not *always* heard. So it was at the advent of the Spirit and the introduction of His new work in the world. That these early manifestations have ceased according to the purpose of God, has been the belief of the most devout saints of all past generations. Yet in these last days when Satan is employing every available issue to confuse and divide the Christian body, to divert their energy and prevent their testimony, there are those who demand a return to Pentecostal manifestations as the only realization of the full ministry of the Spirit. Such professing Christians are bold to condemn the spirituality of saints of all generations who have not accepted their teachings. They are evidently lacking in the knowledge and regard for those gifts which in the Scriptures are said to be of primary importance in contrast to lesser gifts. Whatever is done to revive Pentecostal manifestations should be done in view of *all* that is taught in I Corinthians 14. If God is calling His people to a renewal of all the early manifestations of the Spirit, why is it confined to a little sect, when there are tens of thousands outside that group who are yielded and ready to do His will but are never led into such manifestations? If Satan is using the fact of these early manifestations of the Spirit as an occasion to confuse and divide Christians, all his supernatural power will be displayed and his most subtle deceptions will be imposed to produce what might seem to be the work of God. Many who have been delivered from these "Pentecostal" beliefs and manifestations have since found the more vital things of the Spirit and are deeply concerned for those whom they deem to be yet blinded and self-satisfied in error.

Christian service is not always essential to spirituality. If it is His will for us, we are just as spiritual when resting, playing, ill or infirm as when we are active in service. Our one concern is to know and do His will; but normally, true spirituality is expressed and exercised in the ministries committed to believers and which can be accomplished only by the imparted power of God.

The ministry of restoration is limited to spiritual believers only, according to Galatians 6:1: "Brethren, if a man be overtaken in a fault, ye which are spiritual, restore such an one in the spirit of meekness; considering thyself, lest thou also be tempted." How many heartaches would be avoided if this plain instruction were heeded!

The exact service and individual responsibility of the Christian will never be the same in any two lives and so, in a very real way, no two manifestations of the Spirit will be exactly the same. There is an individual service "foreordained" for each child of God, and there are particular "rivers of living water" to flow from each inner life.

Any Christian may enter into his own "good works," since the enabling Spirit is already indwelling him; but only those who are yielded to God do enter in; for it is service according to *His* will. How little this great fact is appreciated! How often Christians are exhorted to expend more energy and employ all their natural powers with the hope that they may render Christian service! There is evidently a more effectual way to secure the "abiding fruit" in Christian lives. In the Scriptures we read that the "reasonable service," even the "good and acceptable and perfect will of God," is rendered when the child of God presents his whole body to God. Such yielded believers need little exhortation, for the Spirit is mighty through them, and He will employ every available faculty and resource of their lives. Other Christians who are unyielded are little changed by human appeal. Brazen courage enough to force one into fleshly undertakings is not the condition of true Christian service. The one issue is that of a yielded heart and life through which the indwelling Spirit will certainly manifest His mighty power.

Spirituality is not gained by service: it is *unto* service. When one is truly spiritual, all effort is diverted from self struggle to real service. Spirituality is a work of God for His child: service is a work of the child for his God, which can be accomplished only in the power of the indwelling Spirit.

III. THE SPIRIT TEACHES

The teaching manifestation of the Spirit in the believer is described by Christ in John 16:12-15: "I have yet many things to say unto you, but ye cannot bear them now. Howbeit when he, the Spirit of truth, is come, he will guide you into all truth: for he shall not speak of [from] himself; but whatsoever he shall hear, that shall he speak: and he will shew you things to come. He shall glorify me: for he shall receive of mine and shall show it unto you. All things that the Father hath are mine: therefore said I, that he shall take of mine and shall shew it unto you."

Here is a promise that the child of God may enter the highest realm of knowable truth as revealed in the Word of God. "All things that the Father hath" are included in the things of Christ and "things to come," and these form the boundless field into which the believer may be led by the divine Teacher. This storehouse of divine reality will no doubt engage our minds and hearts for ever; but Christians may be even now entering and progressing in these realms of truth and grace. "Now we have received . . . the Spirit which is of God; that we might know the things that are freely given to us of God" (I Corinthians 2:12). "But the anointing which ye have received of him abideth in you, and ye need not that any man teach you: but as the same anointing teacheth you of all things, and is truth, and is no lie, and even as it hath taught you, ye shall abide in him" (I John 2:27).

Beyond all the range of human knowledge there are things "which eye hath not seen, nor ear heard, neither have entered into the heart of man; . . . but God hath revealed them unto us by his Spirit." However, such truth is revealed by the Spirit

only to *spiritual* Christians. To some who were truly saved the
Apostle wrote: "And I, brethren, could not speak unto you as
unto spiritual, but as unto carnal, even as unto babes in Christ.
I have fed you with milk, and not with meat: for hitherto ye
were not able to bear it, neither yet now are ye able" (I
Corinthians 3:1,2). This is a sad disclosure of the state of
some believers. Though born again and possessing the Spirit,
their carnality of life precludes them from understanding, or
progressing in, the "deep things of God." Some, regardless of
educational qualifications, go to the Scriptures of Truth as "those
that find great spoil." His Word, to them, is "sweeter also than
honey and the honey comb." To others, regardless of educational qualifications, there is no discovery and revelation of
Truth. The Bible is read by these as a duty, if read at all. This
is a tragedy in the realm of infinite issues. It is not alone the
question of personal pleasure and profit in the marvels of divine
Truth: it involves the realities of knowledge, or ignorance; obedience, or disobedience for want of understanding; power, or
weakness; helpfulness, or hurtfulness in the life and testimony of
the one who, because of the indwelling Spirit, might be coming
to know and to impart to others something of the boundless
Truth of God. No amount of human education can correct this
defect. The root trouble is *carnality*, and when this is cured,
the "eyes of the heart" will be enlightened, and the inflow of
sanctifying Truth will be continuous and unbroken. "He that is
spiritual discerneth all things."

Christian growth and the deeper knowledge of the Truth are
to be distinguished from spirituality. It is possible to be filled
with the Spirit when immature in growth, experience and understanding. Christian growth is largely conditioned on the study
of the Word, prayer, and service; while spirituality does not
wait on these things, but is conditioned upon immediate adjust-
ments to the Spirit. Since the Spirit is always our Teacher, it is
imperative that we always remain teachable. We should be
willing humbly to hear His voice through any and every
instrument.

IV. THE SPIRIT PROMOTES PRAISE AND THANKSGIVING

Immediately following the injunction of Ephesians 5:18 to be "filled with the Spirit," there is given a description of the normal results of such a filling: "Speaking to yourselves in psalms and hymns and spiritual songs, singing and making melody in your heart to the Lord; giving thanks always for all things unto God and the Father in the name of our Lord Jesus Christ." All things *are* working together for good to the child of God, and it is reasonable that he should give thanks *always* for *all* things. This can be done through the Spirit who knows the "all things" of God. The living creatures in the divine Presence cease not to cry, "Holy! Holy! Holy!" It is equally becoming the heavenly citizen that he render unbroken and endless praise and thanksgiving to God.

It follows, then, that thanksgiving for *all* things and praise unto God are the direct products of the Spirit in the one whom He fills. These great realities are foreign to the finite heart at its best. Not all Christians experience them; but all Christians *may* experience them as certainly as the power has been provided through the indwelling Spirit. The value of this particular manifestation of the Spirit can scarcely be known by the human mind. Praise and thanksgiving are distinctly addressed to God. We cannot know what their full outflow may mean to Him, or what His loss may be when this manifestation is not realized in the believer's life. "Hallelujah!" "Praise ye the Lord!" "Rejoice ever more!"

V. THE SPIRIT LEADS

Since the whole discussion concerning the believer's life in the Spirit, according to the Epistle to the Romans, is consummated in the beginning of the eighth chapter, that which follows in the chapter should be considered as being true only of those who have been adjusted to the larger life and walk in the Spirit. Three distinct manifestations of the Spirit are found in this portion of the Scriptures, and these serve to complete the whole revelation as to the exact work of the Spirit *in* and *through* the one whom He fills.

In Romans 8:14 it is stated: "For as many as are led of the Spirit of God, they are the sons of God." This, it may be concluded, is the normal Christian experience according to the plan and purpose of God. It is equally true that some Christians are abnormal to the extent that they are not constantly led of the Spirit; for it is said also in Galatians 5:18, "But if ye be led of the Spirit, ye are not under the law." The walk in the Spirit, or the life that is led of the Spirit, is one of the great new realities of this age of grace; yet some believers are so far removed from this blessing that their daily lives are shaped and adapted to the order and relationships of the past dispensation. It is one of the supreme glories of this age that the child of God and citizen of heaven may live a superhuman life, in harmony with his heavenly calling, by an unbroken walk in the Spirit. The leading of the Spirit is not experienced by all in whom the Spirit dwells; for such leading must depend on a willingness to go where He, in His infinite wisdom, would have us go.[1]

VI. THE SPIRIT WITNESSETH WITH OUR SPIRIT

In Romans 8:16 it is stated, "The Spirit himself beareth witness with our spirit, that we are the children of God." The primary meaning of this Scripture is that the Spirit witnesseth *with* our spirits unto God. It is also clear that He witnesseth *to* our spirits concerning all that we have in our sonship relation to God. The witnessing work of the Spirit is mentioned again in Galatians 4:6. "And because ye are sons, God hath sent forth the Spirit of his Son into your hearts, crying, Abba, Father." Not only does He actualize this relationship unto us, but He would actualize every great fact which we have taken by faith. "That he would grant you, according to the riches of his glory, to be strengthened with might by his Spirit in the inner man; that Christ may dwell in your hearts by faith; that ye, being rooted and grounded in love, may be able to comprehend with all saints what is the breadth, and length, and depth, and height; and to know the love of Christ, which passeth knowledge, that ye may be filled with all the fulness of God" (Ephesians 3:16-19). "And they

---

[1]See also page 92.

said one to another, Did not our hearts burn within us, while he talked with us by the way, and while he opened to us the scriptures?" The supreme passion of the Apostle Paul was stated in five words: "That I may know him."

By this particular manifestation of the Spirit, unseen things become blessedly real. There is such a thing as "ever learning and never coming to the knowledge of the truth." Truth must become real to us. We may know by faith that we are forgiven and justified forever: it is quite another thing to have a heart experience wherein all is as real as it is true. We may believe in our security and coming glory: it is different to feel its power in the heart. We may believe in "things to come" through the exact teaching of the Word: it is a precious experience to have it made actual to us by the Spirit that "the Lord is at hand," and that our eternal glory with Him may be but a moment removed. Such heart experience is provided in the boundless grace of God for each of His children; but only those who abide in Him can know this ecstasy of life.

VII. THE SPIRIT MAKETH INTERCESSION FOR US

Such a promise is recorded in Romans 8:26 and refers to a particular form of prayer. Intercession must be considered as being limited to that ministry wherein one stands between God and his fellow man. It is simply praying for others. Under those conditions, we know not what to pray for, but the Spirit helpeth our infirmities. Prayer on behalf of others is doubtless the greatest ministry committed to the child of God and a ministry for which he is, and always will be, least prepared within himself. We may become familiar with the truth we preach; but the field of intercession is new, unknown and unknowable. A few Christians have entered this boundless ministry of prayer. Not all have entered; but all Christians *may* enter.

WHAT SPIRITUALITY IS, AND WHAT IT IS NOT

It may be said in conclusion, that a spiritual Christian is a Spirit-filled Christian in whom the unhindered Spirit is manifesting Christ by producing a true Christian character, which is the "fruit of the Spirit"; by energizing true Christian service through the exercise of a "gift of the Spirit"; by personal instruction in the Word of God; by inspiring true praise and thanksgiving; by leading the believer in an unbroken "walk in the Spirit"; by actualizing into celestial heart-ecstasy that which has been taken by faith concerning the positions and possessions in Christ; and by inclining, illuminating and empowering the believer in the prayer of intercession.

True spirituality is a seven-fold manifestation of the Spirit *in* and *through* the one whom He fills. It is a divine output of the life, rather than a mere cessation of things which are called "worldly." True spirituality does not consist in what one does *not* do, it is rather what one *does*. It is not suppression: it is expression. It is not holding in self: it is living out Christ. The unregenerate would not be saved if he should cease sinning: he would not be born of God. The Christian would not be spiritual if he should abstain from worldliness: he would possess none of the manifestations of the Spirit.

The world and "worldly" Christians turn to so-called "worldly" things because they discover in them an anesthetic to deaden the pain of an empty heart and life. The anesthetic, which is often quite innocent in itself, is not so serious a matter as the empty heart and life. Little is gained toward true spirituality when would-be soul doctors have succeeded in persuading the afflicted to get on without the anesthetic. If these instructors do not present the reality of consolation and filling for heart and life which God has provided, the condition will not be improved. How misleading is the theory that to be spiritual one must abandon play, diversion and helpful amusement! Such a conception of spirituality is born of a morbid human conscience. It is foreign to the Word of God. It is a device of Satan to make the blessings of God seem abhorrent to young people who are overflowing with physical life and energy. It is to be regretted that there are those who in blindness are so emphasizing the negatives of the Truth that the impression is created that spirituality is opposed to joy, liberty and naturalness of expression in thought and life in the Spirit. Spirituality is not a pious pose. It is not a "Thou shall *not*": it is "Thou *shalt*." It flings open the doors into the eternal blessedness, energies and resources of God. It is a serious thing to remove the element of relaxation and play from any life. We cannot be normal physically, mentally or spiritually if we neglect this vital factor in human life. God has provided that our joy shall be full.

It is also to be noted that one of the characteristics of true spirituality is that it supersedes lesser desires and issues. The Biblical, as well as practical, cure for "worldliness" among Christians is so to fill the heart and life with the eternal blessings of God that there will be a joyous preoccupation and absent-mindedness to unspiritual things. A dead leaf that may have clung to the twig through the external raging storms of Winter, will silently fall to the ground when the new flow of sap from within has begun in the Spring. The leaf falls because there is a new manifestation of life pressing from within outward. A dead leaf cannot remain where a new bud is springing, nor can worldliness remain where the blessings of the Spirit are flowing. We are not called upon to preach against "dead leaves." We have a message of the imperishable Spring. It is of the outflow of the limitless life of God. When by the Spirit ye are walking ye *cannot* do the things that ye otherwise would.

It is the Spirit's work to produce in the believer a life which is heavenly in character. This life is inimitable; yet it is commonly supposed that spirituality consists in struggling to observe a particular set of rules, or the imitation of a heavenly ideal. Spirituality is not gained by struggling: it is to be *claimed*. It is not *imitation* of a heavenly ideal: it is the *impartation* of the divine power which alone can realize the ideal. "The letter killeth, but the Spirit giveth life." The written Word reveals the character of the spiritual life and exhorts to its fulfilment; but it as faithfully reveals that the life can be lived only by the in-wrought power of God. We are to "serve in newness of spirit, and not in the oldness of the letter." There is little blessing for any Christian until he abandons the principle of living by rules and learns to walk by the Spirit in God-ordained liberty and in fresh and unbroken fellowship with his Lord. The divine precepts will then be kept by the power of God.

SPIRITUALITY A TRIUMPH OF GRACE

In I Corinthians 9:20, 21 the Apostle classifies men in three divisions in view of their relation to the authority of God. He speaks of some who were "under the law": some who are "without law": and himself — a representative of all believers — as neither "under the law" (a Jewish position), nor "without law" (a Gentile position); but "under the law to Christ," which phrase is better translated, "inlawed to Christ." The Epistles abound with many and varied expressions of this latter relationship: "the law of love"; "so fulfil the law of Christ"; "if we keep his commandments"; "stand fast therefore in the liberty wherewith Christ hath made us free, and be not entangled again with the yoke of bondage"; "the law [the yoke of bondage] was given by Moses, but grace and truth came by Jesus Christ." The believer's relation to the divine authority will be found in the fact that he is "inlawed to Christ."

The Bible presents at least three separate and complete rules for daily living.

First, The Law of Moses

Every aspect of the life of an Israelite was anticipated in the law with the statutes and the ordinances. Those governing principles were in effect over Israel, and Israel only, from Moses to Christ (John 1:17).

Second, The Law of the Kingdom

The law of the kingdom incorporates and anticipates the principles of government in the kingdom when it shall be set up in the earth. The body of truth containing this aspect of law is found in the Prophets of the Old Testament, in the preaching of John the Baptist, and in the early teachings of Christ. It is always pure law in character; but in much finer detail. The law of Moses condemned adultery; but the law of the kingdom con-

demns the slightest glance of the eye. The law of Moses condemned murder; but the law of the kingdom condemns a thought
of anger. While the law of Moses is a separate system from
the law of the kingdom, they are alike in the one particular that
they represent only pure law.

Third, The Teachings of Grace

There is a divine counsel for life which is addressed to saved
people of this dispensation. It is the teachings of grace. Grace
teachings represent a complete system for living which covers
every possible contingency in the believer's life and which is
independent and separate from every other system for living
which is found in the Bible. It presents heavenly standards
because it is addressed to born-again heavenly people. There
is much in common between these three complete and separate
bodies of truth and this fact has led some to suppose that the
various commands and injunctions found in all these governing
codes were to be combined into one vast obligation resting upon
the believer. To combine these systems, and to apply them all
to the believer of this age, is to present obligations which are in
themselves, at some points, contradictory and confusing, and to
ignore the vital distinctions between law and grace.

Grace not only presents the divine way of saving and keeping
unworthy sinners: it also *teaches* those who are saved how they
should live. "For the grace of God that bringeth salvation hath
appeared . . . teaching us that, denying ungodliness and worldly
lusts, we should live soberly, righteously, and godly, in this
present world [age]; looking for that blessed hope, and the
glorious appearing of the great God and our Saviour Jesus Christ;
who gave himself for us, that he might redeem us from all iniquity, and purify unto himself a peculiar people, zealous of good
works" (Titus 2:11-14). Grace teachings which anticipate *all*
the walk and warfare of the believer will be found in portions of
the Gospels and The Acts and throughout the Epistles of the New
Testament. It is a complete system and requires no additions
from the law. It incorporates many of the principles which were
in the law, but these are always so restated as to be in exact

harmony with the position and liberty of the one who is "inlawed to Christ."

No Christian is under the law as a rule of life. How often this is stated in the New Testament! It is equally true that no Christian is "without law." This too is the constant theme of the Epistles. Discussions on these themes would cease if all believers understood what it means to be "inlawed to Christ." To be "inlawed to Christ" is to be under the teachings of grace with their provisions for victory. It is not difficult to dismiss the law as a rule of life when we discover that there has been provided another complete system which is in exact harmony with the positions in grace.

There are two aspects of the teachings of grace which are fundamental:

First, they anticipate a manner and quality of life which is superhuman. These standards are none other than "the life which is Christ." In view of the present heavenly position of the redeemed, there could be no less required of them. The Mosaic law, or the law of the kingdom, though complete in themselves as governing principles, and though perfectly fulfilling the mission assigned to them, never aimed at the reproduction of the Christ-life. Their standards, though holy, just and good, are of the earth. In the demands of the law there is no consideration of the most vital activities which are anticipated under grace — prayer, a life of faith, and soul-winning service. The teachings of grace are heavenly and are as far removed from the law as heaven is higher than the earth. The teachings of grace, though presenting a much more difficult standard of living than any law, do not anticipate that the believer will attempt them in his own strength. That would plunge him still deeper into the principle of law with its utter and hopeless failures. Christ is to be perfectly manifested under grace. To this end the most minute details of heavenly conduct are given; but never apart from another and equally age-characterizing fact:

Second, the new life which is "inlawed to Christ" is to be lived by the enabling power of the indwelling Spirit. As has been seen, no help was ever provided under the law. Sin had dominion over law-observers and the law condemned them. Under grace it is provided that "sin shall not have dominion over you." "If ye are led by the Spirit, ye are not under the law." This fact that the enablement for daily life is provided in one case and is not provided in the other is the final and most important distinction between law and grace.

Though not under the law as a rule of life, a Spirit-filled Christian is, however, in a position wherein he cannot do the things which he otherwise would (Galatians 5:17). This again is due to the fact that he is "inlawed to Christ." Being in the power and control of the Spirit, he cannot do the things which he otherwise would do because of the transformed desires of a heart which the Spirit has filled. The power of God is working in such a believer, "both to will and to do of his good pleasure." So, also, the Apostle prays for the Hebrews: "Now the God of peace . . . make you perfect in every good work to do his will, working in you that which is wellpleasing in his sight, through Jesus Christ" (Hebrews 13:20, 21). The Spirit-filled Christians are the only persons in the world who know the blessings of true liberty. Liberty means perfect freedom to do as one is prompted by his own deepest desires. Apart from the energizing power of the Spirit, this liberty may easily become the occasion for the manifestations of the flesh. "For, brethren, ye have been called unto liberty; only use not liberty for an occasion to the flesh, but by love serve one another" (Galatians 5:13). Under grace, the normal Christian is to be Spirit-filled. Thus it is divinely intended and provided that every heart-desire of the child of God shall be prompted by the indwelling Spirit. This is the divine provision for prevailing prayer: "If ye abide in me, and my words abide in you, ye shall ask what ye will, and it shall be done unto you" (John 15:7). Under these definite conditions, the fullest liberty can be granted. It is thus designed that the Spirit-filled Christian is to be free to do in perfect liberty all that his heart prompts him to do; for, when Spirit-filled, he pleases only "to will and to do of his good pleasure." This is "fulfilling the law of Christ." It also fulfils, supersedes, and surpasses all that is contained in any other law. A "carnal" Christian is a violation of all the divine plan and provisions of grace. He is under grace by position only, for he is not yielded to the will and power of God. He is in a state upon which no divine favor can rest, and he is falling short of the marvels of divine grace.

It should never be concluded that the life in grace is circumscribed and narrow. This is the view which is taken by both the "natural man" to whom the things of the Spirit are only "foolishness," and the "carnal" man who "cannot bear" spiritual things. Neither the "natural man" nor the "carnal" man should ever be expected to understand the triumph of the spiritual life in grace. The glory of these divine realities have too long been confused and distorted by the opinions of such men.

To be "inlawed to Christ" is to enter the door into the things which are infinite. It is like the exit of the grub from the dark confinements of the chrysalis state into the glorious sun-kissed, world-wide, heaven-high freedom of the butterfly. The butterfly needs no law to prohibit him from returning to the former state; but sadly indeed do we discover that there is the presence in us of the flesh which must be kept in all subjection by the power of God. For this victory our God is sufficient.

We are told to stand fast in the blessed liberty in Christ. Our liberty consists not only in the freedom from the law, but also in the fact of the quickening and enabling power of the Spirit. Apart from whole dependence upon God we shall be entangled in fleshly efforts which is a return to the principles and requirements of the law. How important is the injunction, "Be filled with the Spirit"! How great is the contrast between human nothingness and divine sufficiency — the one just as real as the other!

It is possible to be born of the Spirit, baptized with the Spirit, indwelt by the Spirit, and sealed with the Spirit and yet to be without the filling of the Spirit. The first four of these ministries are already perfectly accomplished in every believer from the moment he is saved; for they depend upon the faithfulness of the Father to His child. The last of these ministries, the filling of the Spirit, has not been experienced by every Christian; for it depends on the faithfulness of the child to his Father.

Spirituality is not gained in answer to prevailing prayer; for there is little Scripture to warrant the believer to be praying for the filling of the Spirit. It is the *normal* work of the Spirit to fill the one who is rightly adjusted to God. The Christian will always be filled while he is making the work of the Spirit possible in his life.[1]

---

[1]In a review of the first edition of this book, which appeared in *The Princeton Theological Review* for April, 1919, the reviewer, Dr. Benjamin B. Warfield, D.D., objects to this statement, and to all similar teachings in this book. This teaching, he points out, "subjects the gracious working of God to human determination." Is this teaching Biblical?

The Scripture gives unquestionable emphasis to the sovereignty of God. God has perfectly determined what will be, and His determined purpose will be realized; for it is impossible that God should ever be either surprised or disappointed. So, also, there is equal emphasis in the Scriptures upon the fact that lying between these two undiminished aspects of His sovereignty — His eternal purpose and its perfect realization — He has permitted sufficient latitude for some exercise of the human will. In so doing, His determined ends are in no way jeopardized. There is difficulty here, but what, in Scripture, is difficult for the finite mind to harmonize, is doubtless harmonized in the mind of God.

Though it is revealed that God must impart the moving, enabling grace whereby one may believe unto salvation (John 6:44, cf. 12:32), or whereby one may yield unto a spiritual life (Philippians 2:13), it is as clearly revealed that, within His sovereign purpose and power, God has everywhere conditioned both salvation and the spiritual life upon these human conditions. Both believing and yielding are presented as injunctions. The fact that "No man can come to me, except the Father which hath sent me draw him" is invariably true; yet it is equally true that some resourcefulness of the human will, though it be divinely enabled, is appealed to by the words, "Believe on the Lord Jesus Christ, and thou shalt be saved." So, again: "This is the will of God, even your sanctification," is a revelation which is invariably true; yet it is equally true that the believer's will is appealed to when he is besought to "yield himself unto God." One aspect of this truth without the other will lead, in the one case, to fatalism, wherein there is no place for petition in prayer, no motive for the wooing of God's love, no ground for condemnation, no occasion for evangelistic appeal, and no meaning to very much Scripture: in the other case, it will lead to the dethroning of God. Though the will be moved upon by the enabling power of God, spirituality, according to God's Word, is made to depend upon that divinely-enabled human choice; Romans 12:1, 2; Galatians 5:16; Ephesians 4:30; I Thessalonians 5:19 and I John 1:9 being sufficient evidence. Men are said to be "condemned" "because

So, also, spirituality, or the filling of the Spirit, does not depend upon patient waiting. The disciples waited ten days for the advent of the Spirit into the world, and He came as they were taught to expect. They were not waiting for their own personal filling alone; but rather for the whole new ministry of the Spirit

---

they have not believed" (John 3:18), and sin will reign in the Christian's life unless the appeal is heeded: "Let not sin therefore reign in your mortal body." To state that spirituality is made possible, on the human side, by well-defined human acts and attitudes may seem "a quite terrible expression" (to quote the reviewer) as viewed by an arbitrary theological theory; however, it is evidently Biblical.

The same reviewer objects to the teaching that there is any sudden change possible from the carnal state to the spiritual state. To quote: "He who believes in Jesus Christ is under grace, and his whole course, in its process and in its issue alike, is determined by grace, and therefore, having been predestined to be conformed to the image of God's Son, he is surely being conformed to that image, God Himself seeing to it that he is not only called and justified but also glorified. You may find Christians at every stage of this process, for it is a process through which all must pass; but you will find none who will not in God's own good time and way pass through every stage of it. There are not two kinds of Christians, although there are Christians at every conceivable stage of advancement towards the one goal to which all are bound and at which all shall arrive."

Doubtless there are varying degrees of carnality as there are varying degrees of spirituality, but the positive denial of the statement that there are two well-defined classes of believers — "carnal" and "spiritual" — would be better supported by conclusive exposition of a large body of Scripture in which this two-fold classification of Christians seems to be taught.

In this reviewer's mind, the change from carnality to spirituality is evidently confused with Christian growth. Christian growth is undoubtedly a process of development under the determined purpose of God which will end, with the certainty of the Infinite, in a complete likeness to Christ; but spirituality is the present state of blessing and power of the believer who, at the same time, may be very immature. A Christian can and should be spiritual from the moment he is saved. Spirituality, which is the unhindered manifestations of the Spirit in life, is provided to the full for *all* believers who "confess" their sins, "yield" to God, and "walk not after the flesh, but after the Spirit." When these conditions are complied with, the results are *immediate*; for no process is indicated. Jacob, an Old Testament type, was completely changed in one night.

Christian experience bears unfailing testimony to two outstanding facts: (1) There is an abrupt change from the carnal to the spiritual when the Biblical conditions are met. And (2) there is an abrupt loss of spiritual blessing whenever there has been a yielding to sin.

to begin, as it did on the Day of Pentecost. When He came, all who were prepared in heart and life were instantly filled with the Spirit and no believer has had occasion to *wait* for the Spirit since that day.

Neither prayer nor waiting, therefore, are conditions of spirituality.

Of the three Biblical conditions upon which a Christian may be spiritual, or Spirit-filled, two are directly connected with the issue of sin in the believer's daily life, and one with the yielding of the will to God. These three conditions are now to be considered.

> "Our blest Redeemer, ere He breathed
>   His tender last farewell,
> A Guide, a Comforter, bequeathed
>   With us to dwell.
>
> "And every virtue we possess,
>   And every victory won,
> And every thought of holiness,
>   Are His alone."

CHAPTER 4

"GRIEVE NOT THE HOLY SPIRIT"

THE FIRST CONDITION OF TRUE SPIRITUALITY

CHRISTIANS ARE APPOINTED to live every moment of their lives with the Holy Spirit of God. Life for them is a moment by moment vital union with One who is infinitely holy. Sin, therefore, in a Christian, is the very opposite of any true manifestation of the Spirit in the life.

WHAT IT IS THAT GRIEVES THE SPIRIT

Sin destroys spirituality. It is necessarily so; for where sin is tolerated in the believer's daily life, the Spirit, who indwells him, must then turn from His blessed ministry *through* him, to a pleading ministry *to* him. The Bible does not teach that the Spirit withdraws because of sin in the one whom He indwells: He is rather *grieved* by the sin.

A child of God lives either with a grieved or an ungrieved Spirit. It may reasonably be questioned, in the light of God's Word, whether the saved person, having received the Spirit, ever lives by the dictates of his conscience. The standards of human conscience must give way to a standard of moral judgment which is infinitely higher. A Christian's manner of life either grieves or does not grieve the Holy Spirit of God. The Apostle Paul writes of the fact that his conscience bore him witness in the Holy Spirit, and it is quite probable that the Spirit uses the conscience as a human faculty; but He as certainly imparts to it the new standard of the infinite holiness of God. The injunction to the one in whom the Spirit dwells is,

"And grieve not the Holy Spirit of God whereby ye are sealed unto the day of redemption" (Ephesians 4:30).

A true spiritual life must depend then, to a large degree, upon the right understanding and adjustment concerning the issues of sin in the believer's daily life. About this God has spoken explicitly, and it will be found that the Bible teaching on the subject of the sins of Christians is twofold: (1) God has provided that the sin of His child may be *prevented*,[1] and (2) He has also provided that the effect of sin, if it has been committed, may be *cured*. It is imperative that this two-fold classification of the purpose of God in dealing with sin in His children be recognized.

THE CURE OF THE EFFECTS OF SIN IN A CHRISTIAN

Having sinned, what must a Christian do? What is the divine condition for the cure of the havoc of sin in the spirituality of the believer? No attempt should be made here to name sins which hinder the Spirit. He is grieved by any, and all, sin, and He is abundantly able to convince the one in whom He dwells of the particular sin, or sins, which grieve Him. So, also, it is an issue only of *known* sin; for no person can deal intelligently with unknown sin. This first condition of true spirituality is centered upon *definite* matters. It is sin that has, by the grieving of the Spirit, become a distinct issue; for the term "grieving the Spirit" refers as much to the heart experience of the one in whom He dwells as to the personal attitude of the Spirit toward sin. The issue is, therefore, a well-defined wrong, about which the child of God has been made conscious by the Spirit. Such *known* sin must be dealt with according to the exact direction of the Word of God.

Should spiritual darkness be experienced apart from the consciousness of any particular sin having been committed, it is the privilege of the Christian to pray for a clearer understanding. Physical conditions very often enter into the mental state and when this is true it is most misleading to suppose that a morbid or unhappy state of mind is necessarily a result of sin. If one is

[1]See Chapter 6.

conscious of the fact that he is depleted in nerve strength, or is physically depressed, allowance should be made for that fact.

In the Bible, the divine offer and condition for the cure of sin in an unsaved person is crystallized into one word, *"believe"*; for the forgiveness of sin with the unsaved is only offered as an indivisible part of the whole divine work of salvation. The saving work of God includes many mighty undertakings other than the forgiveness of sin, and salvation depends only upon *believing*. It is not possible to separate some one issue from the whole work of His saving grace, such as forgiveness, and claim this apart from the indivisible whole. It is, therefore, a grievous error to direct an unsaved person to seek forgiveness of his sins as a separate issue. A sinner minus his sins would not be a Christian; for salvation is more than subtraction: it is addition. "I give unto them eternal life." Thus the sin question with the unsaved will be cured as a part of, but never separate from, the whole divine work of salvation, and this salvation depends upon *believing*.

In like manner, also, in the Bible, the divine offer and condition of cure for the effects of sin in the Christian's life is crystallized into one word, *"confess."* The vital meaning of this one word and its bearing on the question of the cure of sin in a child of God is an important, though much neglected, doctrine of the Word of God. The way back to blessing for a sinning saint is the same, whether before the cross, or after the cross, and the Bible teaching on the restoration of a believer is contained in seven major passages.

THE SEVEN MAJOR PASSAGES

FIRST, CHRIST ALONE CAN CLEANSE FROM SIN (John 13:1-11)

The fact that the sins of Christians must be cleansed by Christ alone is revealed in John 13:1-11. The passage is at the very beginning of the Upper Room Conversation. A few hours before, Christ had given His farewell address to the nation Israel; but in the upper room He is speaking His farewell words to His disciples, not as Jews, but as those who are "clean every whit." Of them He also said, "Now ye are clean through the word which I have spoken unto you." In this conversation He is anticipating the new conditions and relationships which were to obtain after His cross (John 16:4). It is important to note that His first teaching concerning a Christian's present relationship to God was concerning the cleansing of defilement, thus signifying its importance in the divine estimation. The way of salvation has been revealed in the preceding chapters of this Gospel; but beginning with chapter thirteen, He is speaking to those who are saved, and speaking to them of the divine cleansing from their defilement.

He arose from supper, laid aside His outer garments, girded Himself with a towel (the insignia of a servant), poured water into a basin and began to wash the disciples' feet. This is a miniature of a much larger undertaking, when He arose from the fellowship with His Father in heaven and laid aside the garments of His glory and humbled Himself, taking the form of a servant and became obedient unto death, even the death of the cross, in order that we might be washed with the washing of regeneration (Titus 3:5). In the larger undertaking there is the whole cleansing: in the other there is a partial cleansing which is typified by the cleansing of the feet only of the one who is otherwise "clean every whit."

This two-fold cleansing was also typified by the prescribed cleansing for the Old Testament priest. When he entered his ministry he was given a ceremonial bath, which was of his whole body, *once for all* (Exodus 29:4). Yet he was required to bathe his hands and feet at the brazen laver before every ministry and service (Exodus 30:17-21). So the New Testament believer, though once for all cleansed as to his salvation, must also be cleansed from every defilement, and Christ alone can make him clean.

SECOND, CONFESSION IS THE ONE CONDITION OF FELLOWSHIP, FORGIVENESS AND CLEANSING (I John 1:1 to 2:2)

I John 1:1 to 2:2 is the second major passage concerning the Father's dealing with His children who have sinned. John, the expert witness with regard to the blessedness of unbroken communion and fellowship with the Father and with His Son, writes these things that we also may have fellowship. "God is light," or perfect holiness. If we should say that we have fellowship with Him and are, nevertheless, walking in darkness (sin), we lie and do not the truth. On the other hand, if we walk in the light, as He is in the light, we have fellowship with the Father and with His Son Jesus Christ. Sinless perfection is not demanded by this passage. It is not a command for the Christian to *become* the light, or what God alone is: it is rather that there may be an immediate adjustment to the light which God has shed into the life by the Spirit. He has required of us *confession*. When He convinces us of sin, or is grieved by sin, that sin is to be dealt with *at once*. The passage goes on to state that there is only one condition for the cure of the effect of sin in the believer's life: "If we confess our sins, he is faithful and just to forgive us our sins, and to cleanse us from all unrighteousness" (v. 9). It is not *mercy* and *kindness*: He is *faithful* and *just* to forgive, and it is all granted on the one condition of *confession*. He is *"faithful"* to His child; for we are dealing always and only with our Father (2:2). He is *"just"* because the atoning blood has been shed to cover the condemning power of every sin (John 5:24). Thus in perfect righteousness the Father's forgiveness is exercised toward His child.

Divine forgiveness is never an act of leniency. God can righteously forgive only when the full satisfaction of His holiness has been met. The root meaning of the word forgive, in the Scriptures, is *remission*. It represents the divine act of separating the sin from the sinner. Human forgiveness is merely a lifting of the penalty: divine forgiveness is exercised only when the penalty, according to the terms of His infinite righteousness, has first been executed on the sinner, or his Substitute. This was true in the Old Testament: "The priest shall make an atonement for his sin that he hath committed, and it shall be forgiven him" (Leviticus 4:35). The forgiveness was possible with God, only when there had been a full atonement for sin. So in the New Testament, or after the sacrifice has been made at the cross for us, we are told that the blood of Christ *has* become the sufficient atonement for our sins. "This is my blood of the new testament, which is shed for many for the remission of sins" (Matthew 26:28). All divine forgiveness whether toward the unsaved or the saved, is now based on the shed blood of Christ. His blood answers the last demand of a holy God. When we were saved He forgave us "all trespasses" (Colossians 2:13). This is *judicial* forgiveness and means the removal of the grounds of condemnation *forever*. There is still *parental* forgiveness to be exercised toward the sinning child. It is not exercised in order to rescue the child from destruction and condemnation; but it is exercised in order to restore him from a state wherein he is out of fellowship, into the full blessing of communion with the Father and with His Son. It is wholly within the family circle and the restoration is unto the full enjoyment of those blessings. It is not restoration to *sonship*, — of that the Bible knows nothing. It is restoration to *fellowship*.

The defilement of a Christian may be forgiven and cleansed on the one condition of a confession which is prompted by true heart-repentance. We are not forgiven our sins because we *ask* to be forgiven. It is when we *confess* our sins that we are forgiven. It will not do to substitute prayer for confession, though prayer may be the means of expressing a true sorrow for sin. Multitudes are praying for forgiveness who have made no confession of their sin. There is no Scripture for the child of God under grace which justifies such a substitution.

The truth embodied in this passage cannot apply to unsaved people. They are forgiven as a part of their whole salvation when they *believe*. The child of God is forgiven when he makes a full *confession*.

THIRD, SELF-JUDGMENT SAVES FROM CHASTISEMENT (I Corinthians 11:31, 32)

The third major passage related to the cure of the effects of sin in the believer's life is found (without reference to the important context) in I Corinthians 11:31, 32: "For if we would judge ourselves, we should not be judged. But when we are judged, we are chastened of the Lord, that we should not be condemned with the world." The important additional revelation gained from this passage, is in the order it discloses. The Father is here seen to be waiting for the self-judgment, or confession, of His sinning child; but if the child will not judge himself by a full confession of his sin, then the Father must judge him. When the child is thus judged by the Father, he is chastened. This, it should be noted, is with a definite purpose in view: "That we should not be condemned with the world." There may be chastisement for the child of God; but there can be no condemnation. His wonderful grace as a Father is seen in His willingness to wait until His child has judged himself; but as a righteous Father, He cannot pass over the unconfessed sin of His child. If self-judgment is neglected, He must administer chastisement.

FOURTH, CHASTISEMENT IS THE FATHER'S CORRECTION AND TRAINING OF HIS SINNING CHILD (Hebrews 12:3-15)

The central passage in the Bible on chastisement is found in Hebrews 12:3-15 and should be included as one of the major passages upon the cure of the effect of sin in a Christian's life. By this Scripture we understand that chastisement is the Father's correction of *every* child; for He has said, "whom the Lord loveth he chasteneth," and, in chastisement, "God dealeth with you as with sons." Such correction as is accomplished by chastisement has in view "that we might be partakers of his holiness."[1] Chastisement is more than correction and punishment. The meaning of the word includes training and development. It therefore may be administered by the Father for the teaching, refining and training of the child.

Light is given us in God's revelation as to what general form His chastisement may take. It is reasonable to conclude that the Father deals individually with His children and that His ways are manifold.

In I Corinthians 11:30 we read concerning the judgments of the Father because of sin in His children: "For this cause many

---

[1]See also page 94.

are weak and sickly among you, and many sleep." Weakness, sickliness and even death may then be included within those means which the Father may employ with His unyielding child. It must not be concluded that *all* weakness, sickliness and death among believers is a chastisement from God. The passage teaches that chastisement may take these particular forms.

In John 15:1-17 there is teaching concerning the importance of abiding in Christ. This is but another term meaning the life of true spirituality. In this Scripture some of the results of not abiding in Christ are disclosed. The branch that does not bear fruit is lifted up out of its place. It does not cease to be a branch; but is evidently taken from this relationship to be "with the Lord." This statement corresponds with the statement that "many sleep." Failure to abide in Christ results, also, in loss of effectiveness in prayer, loss of power in fruit-bearing and service, and loss of joy and fellowship in the Lord.[1]

The very weight of the hand of God may be exceedingly heavy. David describes his experience when he "kept silence," or refused to acknowledge his sin: "When I kept silence, my bones waxed old through my roaring all the day long. For day and night thy hand was heavy upon me: my moisture is turned into the drought of summer. I acknowledge my sin unto thee, and my iniquity have I not hid. I said, I will confess my transgression unto the LORD; and thou forgavest the iniquity of my sin. For this shall every one that is godly pray unto thee in a time when thou mayest be found" (Psalm 32:3-6).

The weight of the hand of God is like an unceasing ache of the soul. It is none other than a grieved Spirit; but His loving hand may be still heavier in correction if we fail to say as did David: "I acknowledge my sin unto thee."[1]

FIFTH, AN EXAMPLE OF CHRISTIAN REPENTANCE (II Corinthians 7:8-11)

In II Corinthians 7:8-11 an example of true sorrow for sin on the part of a Christian is recorded. The Apostle, in his first

---

[1]See also page 90.
[1]See also Chapter 4.

letter to the Corinthians, has been used of the Spirit to convince them of sin, and in this fifth major passage we are given an account of their sorrow for sin and the effect of this sorrow in their lives. Much light is here given on the transforming effect of repentance and confession in a Christian's life. The passage follows: "For though I made you sorry with a letter, I do not repent, though I did repent: for I perceive that the same epistle hath made you sorry, though it were but for a season. Now I rejoice, not that ye were made sorry, but that ye sorrowed to repentance: for ye were made sorry after a godly manner, that ye might receive damage by us in nothing. For godly sorrow worketh repentance to salvation not to be repented of: but the sorrow of the world worketh death. For behold the self-same thing, that ye sorrowed with a godly sort, what carefulness it wrought in you, yea, what clearing of yourselves, yea, what indignation, yea, what fear, yea, what vehement desire, yea, what zeal, yea, what revenge!"

Such is the transforming power and abiding effect of true repentance and confession in the life of a believer.

SIXTH, THE REPENTANCE, CONFESSION AND RESTORATION OF AN OLD TESTAMENT SAINT (Psalm 51:1-19)

As recorded in Psalm 51, David is the outstanding example of true repentance and confession on the part of an Old Testament saint. In the Scriptures his sin is laid bare and with it his broken and contrite heart. He was saved (howbeit under the Old Testament relationships); for he prayed, "Restore unto me the joy of thy salvation." He did not pray, restore unto me my salvation. He knew that his salvation, which depended only on the faithfulness of God, had not failed. He was pleading for a return of the joy which had been lost through sin. He had lost his testimony as well. Anticipating his restoration he said, "Then will I teach transgressors thy ways; and sinners shall be converted unto thee."

Being saved, even though of the Old Testament order, David's way back to God was by way of *confession*. There are portions of this major passage which, although true of an Old Testament saint, could not be rightly applied to a Christian in this new dispensation of Grace. We need never pray, "And take not thy Holy Spirit from me"; for He has come to abide. So, also, we need not plead for forgiveness and restoration. Since the blood has been shed on the cross, the blessings of forgiveness and cleansing are instantly bestowed through the faithfulness and justice of God upon the believer who makes a full *confession.*

SEVENTH, THE THREE-FOLD ILLUSTRATIVE PARABLE IN THE GOS-
PELS (Luke 15:1-32)

The last of the seven major passages bearing on the cure of the effects of sin upon the spiritual life of a saint, whether of the Old Testament, or the New, is found in Luke 15:1-32. This portion of the Scriptures contains one parable in three parts. It is of a lost sheep, a lost piece of silver, and a lost son. Though three incidents are told, there is but one underlying purpose. The particular value of this passage, in the present connection, is in its revelation of the divine compassion as seen in the restoration of a sinning saint. It is the unveiling of the Father's heart. The emphasis falls upon the shepherd, rather than upon the sheep; upon the woman, rather than upon the lost piece of silver; and upon the father, rather than upon either son.

In considering this passage, it must be borne in mind that what is here recorded is under the conditions which obtained before the cross. It, therefore, has to do primarily with Israel. They were the covenant people of the Old Testament, "the sheep of his pasture," and their position as such was unchanged until the new covenant was made in His blood. Being covenant people, they could return to the blessings of their covenant, if those blessings had been lost through sin, on the grounds of repentance and confession. This, according to the Scriptures and as has been seen, is true of all covenant people. Israel's covenants are not the same in character as "the new covenant made in his blood"; but the terms of restoration into the blessings of the covenant are the same in the one case as in the other. The *fact* of the covenant abides through the faithfulness of God; but the *blessings* of the covenant may be lost through the unfaithfulness of the saint. The blessing is regained, too, not by forming another covenant, but by restoration into the unchanging privileges of the original covenant.

The three-fold parable is about Israelites and was addressed to them. Whatever application there may be in the parable to Christians under the new covenant is possible only on the ground of the fact that the way of restoration by repentance and confession is common to both covenants. In the parable, therefore, we have a picture of the heart of God toward any and all of His covenant people when they sin.

The parable opens thus: "Then drew near unto him all the publicans and sinners for to hear him. And the Pharisees and scribes murmured, saying, This man receiveth sinners, and eateth with them." Here is the key to all that follows. "Publicans and sinners" were not Gentiles. Publicans were Israelites under the covenant "made unto the fathers" who had turned traitor to their nation to the extent of becoming tax-gatherers for Rome. "Sinners" were Israelites under the same covenant who had failed to present the sacrifices for sin as prescribed by the law of Moses. An Israelite was counted "blameless" before the law when he had provided the required offerings. Thus Paul could say of himself concerning his former position as a Jew under the law: "Touching the righteousness which is in the law, blameless." The Apostle is not claiming sinless perfection: he is testifying to the fact that he had always been faithful in providing the sacrifices prescribed in the law of Moses. The Pharisees and scribes were Israelites who gave their whole lives to the exact fulfillment of the law of Moses. Paul was a Pharisee, "an Hebrew of the Hebrews." These men were not Christians and should not be judged as such. There is little in common here with Christians. These Israelites were blameless through the animal sacrifices which anticipated the death of Christ. Christians are blameless through faith in the blood of Christ which has already been shed. One is a justification by works, on the human side; the other is a justification by faith concerning a finished work of God.

The Pharisees and scribes murmured when they saw that Jesus received publicans and sinners and ate with them. He, therefore, spoke this parable unto *them*. The parable is explicitly addressed to murmuring Pharisees and scribes rather than to everybody, anywhere. And there can be little understanding of the truth contained in it unless the plain purpose for which it is told is kept in mind.

In turning to an interpretation of the parable, some consideration must be given to the well-nigh universal impression that this parable is a picture of salvation. While it is a blessed picture of the heart of God, it most evidently had to do with *restoration* rather than *regeneration*.

The first division of the parable is of a man who had an hundred sheep. "What man of you, having an hundred sheep, if he lose one of them, doth not leave the ninety and nine in the wilderness, and go after that which is lost, until he find it?" This is not a picture of ninety-nine sheep and one goat: it is of one hundred sheep, and "sheep," according to the Scriptures, are always covenant people. Israelites were sheep, so, also, are the Christians of this dispensation. Jesus, when speaking of those to be saved through His death, said to the Jews: "Other sheep I have which are not of this fold" (John 10:16).

Another important distinction should be noted in this parable: The sheep, the piece of silver and the son were *"lost"*; but they were lost in such a way as that they needed to be *"found."* This is hardly the same as being *lost* in such a way as needing to be *saved*. The Biblical use of the word "lost" has at least these two widely different meanings. "The Son of Man has come to seek and to save that which was lost"; but in all three parts of this parable, it is seeking and *finding*, rather than seeking and *saving*. The word *"saved,"* it should be observed, does not once appear in this parable. Should this parable be accepted as a teaching in regard to salvation, there is no escaping the error of "universalism"; for this Shepherd seeks *until* He finds that which is lost. The passage, on the other hand, presents a blessed unfolding of the heart of God toward His wandering child who needs to be *found* rather than to be *saved*. "Ninety and nine" who are safe in the fold to one that is lost is a poor picture of the proportions which have always existed between the saved and unsaved. Were the parable to teach the salvation of a sinner, far better would it have been had it presented "ninety and nine" who were lost to one that was safe in the fold. The parable continues:

"And when he hath found it, he layeth it on his shoulders, rejoicing. And when he cometh home, he calleth together his friends and neighbours, saying unto them, Rejoice with me; for I have found my sheep which was lost. I say unto you, that likewise joy shall be in heaven over one sinner that repenteth, more than over ninety and nine just persons, which need no repentance."

The sinner here referred to can be none other than one of the covenant sinners of the first verse of the passage and concerning whom the parable was told. He, being a covenant person, is here pictured by the Spirit as returning on the grounds of repentance, rather than being saved on the grounds of saving faith. So, again, we could hardly find any class of persons within the church corresponding to the "ninety and nine just persons who need no repentance." Such a case was possible, nevertheless, under the law of Moses, the Apostle Paul being a good example. The very Pharisees and scribes to whom the parable was addressed were of that class. Within the outward demands of the law of Moses, they needed no repentance.

Repentance, which means a change of mind, is a vital element in our present salvation; but it is now *included* in the one act of believing; for fully one hundred and fifty passages in the New Testament condition our present salvation on *believing*, or its synonym, *faith*. The Gospel by John, written especially that we might believe that Jesus is the Christ and that believing we might have life through His name, does not once use the word "*repentance*." The unsaved today are saved through *believing*, which evidently includes such repentance as can be produced by those who are "dead in trespasses and sins." Repentance means a change of mind and no one can believe on Christ as his Saviour and not have changed his mind with respect to his sin, his lost condition and the placing of his saving trust in the One who is "mighty to save."

The second division of the parable is of the woman and the lost piece of silver. It is the same story of *seeking* and *finding* that which was lost. The special emphasis in this division of the parable falls on the *joy* of the one who *finds*. It is the joy of the One in whose presence the angels are. The story, again, is of a *repenting* sinner, rather than of a *believing* sinner.

The third division of the parable is of "*A certain man.*" This story is evidently told to reveal the heart of the father. Incidentally he had two sons, and one of them was a "publican and sinner," and the other a "Pharisee and scribe." One left the blessings of his father's house (but did not cease to be a son): the other *murmured* when the sinner was restored.

No greater depths of degradation could be pictured to a Jewish mind than to be found in a field feeding swine. Here we have the Lord declaring, in the terms of His own time and people, that a wandering *son* may return by confession, even from the lowest depths of sin. It was there, in that field with the swine, that the son "came to himself" and purposed to return to his father with a confession, which is only the normal expression of a true heart-repentance. There is no mention of regeneration. Nothing is said of faith, apart from which no soul could hope to be saved into sonship. He was a *son* and returned to his father as a *son*. The sentiment, that an unsaved person, when turning to Christ, is "returning home" as is sometimes expressed in sermons and gospel songs, is foreign to the teachings of the Word of God. Sons, who have wandered away, may return home, and, being *lost* in the state of wandering, may be *found*. This could not apply to one who has never been a child of God. Such are certainly *lost* but need rather to be *saved*. In this dispensation, unsaved people may *turn* to God, but they do not *return* to God.

When the returning son was a great way off the father saw him and had compassion on him and ran and fell on his neck and kissed him. The father saw him because he was looking that way. He had not ceased to look since the hour the son departed. Such is the picture of the Father's heart, expressed, as well, in the searching both by the shepherd and by the woman.

All righteousness would require that this returning boy be punished most severely. Had he not dishonored the father's name? Had he not squandered his father's substance? Had he not brought himself to ruin? But he was not punished. The fact that he was not punished unfolds to us of this dispensation the blessed truth that, because of the work of Christ on the cross, the Father can and will receive His child without punishment. The terms of restoration are only a broken-hearted confession. The *guilt* of the sin has fallen on Another in our stead.

The confession of this son was first toward heaven and then to his father. This is the true order of all confession. It must be first to God and then to those who would be wronged by the withholding of our confession.

Great is the power of a broken-hearted confession. No one would believe that the wandering son, after having been restored, and after resting again in the comforts of that fellowship and home, would immediately ask his father for more of his goods that he might return to the life of sin. Such action would be wholly inconsistent with the heart-broken confession he has made. True confession is real and transforming in its power (see II Corinthians 7:11).

He was a *son* during all the days of his absence from home. Had he died in the field with the swine, he would have died as a *son*. So far as this illustrates the estate of a sinning Christian, it may be concluded from this and all the Scriptures on this subject, that an imperfect Christian, such as we all are, would be received into the heavenly home at death, though he suffers loss of all rewards and much joy, and though, when he meets his Lord face to face he is called upon there to make his hitherto neglected confession.

From these seven major passages it may be concluded that the cure of the effects of sin on the spiritual life of a child of God is promised to the one who in repentance of heart makes a genuine confession of his sin.

Sin is always sin in the sight of God. It is no less sin because it is committed by a Christian, nor can it be cured in any case other than through the redemption which is in Christ. It is because the redemption-price has already been paid in the precious blood of Christ that God can save sinners who only *believe* and restore saints who only *confess*. Not one degree of the punishment that fell upon our Substitute can ever fall on saint or sinner. Since Christ bore it all for us, believing or confessing is all that can righteously be demanded. Until confession is made by the one who has sinned, he is contending for that which is evil and thus is at disagreement with the Father. "Two cannot walk together except they be agreed." God cannot agree with sin. The child can agree with the Father and this is true repentance which is expressed in true confession. Repentance is a change of mind. By it we turn from sin unto God.

The blessing does not depend upon sinless perfection: it is a matter of not grieving the Spirit. It is not an issue concerning *unknown* sin: it is an attitude of heart that is willing always instantly to confess every *known* sin. "If we confess our sins, he is faithful and just to forgive us our sins, and to cleanse us from all unrighteousness." The Christian who fully confesses all *known* sin will have removed one, if not all, of the hindrances to the fullest manifestation of the Spirit.

"And grieve not the holy Spirit of God, whereby ye are sealed unto the day of redemption" (Ephesians 4:30).

CHAPTER 5

"QUENCH NOT THE SPIRIT"

THE SECOND CONDITION OF TRUE SPIRITUALITY

"QUENCH NOT THE SPIRIT" (I Thessalonians 5:19) is another explicit command to the believer concerning his relation to the One who indwells him.

WHAT IS IT THAT QUENCHES THE SPIRIT?

The Spirit is "quenched" by any unyieldedness to the revealed will of God. It is simply saying "no" to God, and so is closely related to matters of the divine appointments for service; though the Spirit may be "quenched," as well, by any resistance of the providence of God in the life.

The word "quench," when related to the Spirit, does not imply that He is extinguished, or that He withdraws: it is rather the act of *resisting* the Spirit. The Spirit does not remove His presence. He has come to abide.

According to the Scriptures, the believer's responsibility in realizing true spirituality is again crystallized into one crucial word, *"yield."* "But yield yourselves unto God, as those that are alive from the dead, and your members as instruments of righteousness unto God" (Romans 6:13). Such an attitude of heart toward the will of God becomes those who "are alive from the dead," and any other attitude is no less than rebellion in the family and household of God. Our Father is never mistaken. His will is always infinitely best. Therefore we must not "quench the Spirit." We must not say *"no"* to God.

When we have entered heaven by His grace, and have gained the larger vision and understanding of that sphere, we shall look back over our pilgrim pathway on the earth and have either joy, or regret, as we contemplate the life we have lived. There is a life of no regrets. It consists in having done the will of God. That divine plan and purpose will be recognized through all eternity as that which was God's very best for us.

THE YIELDED LIFE

To be yielded to Him is to allow Him to design and execute the position and effectiveness of our life. He alone can do this. Of all the numberless paths in which we might walk, He alone knows which is best. He alone has power to place our feet in that path and to keep them there, and He alone has love for us that will never cease to prompt Him to do for us all that is in His wisdom, power and love to do. Truly the life is thrice blessed that learns to yield to the will of God.

Nothing could be more misdirected than a self-directed life. In our creation God has purposely omitted any faculty, or power, of self-direction. "O LORD, I know that the way of man is not in himself: it is not in man that walketh to direct his steps" (Jeremiah 10:23). It is the divine plan that the element of guidance shall be supplied in us by God Himself. One of the results of the Adamic fall is the independence of the human will toward God; yet man is most spiritual and most conformed to the design of his Maker when he is most yielded to the divine will. What greater evidence of the fall do we need than that we must struggle to be yielded to Him? How much we feel we have gained when we can say, "Thy will, not mine be done"! It is because our daily life will be helpless and a failure apart from the leading of the Spirit, and because the Spirit has come to do this very work, that we cannot be rightly adjusted to Him, or be spiritual, until we are yielded to the mind and will of God.

A full dedication of our bodies to be a "living sacrifice" is the "reasonable service" and is an issue of first importance for the child of God. Following the doctrinal statement of the two-fold work of God for us in our salvation, as recorded in Romans, chapters 1-8, and after the dispensational portion of the Epistle concerning Israel, the message of the book turns at chapter 12 to an appeal for the manner of life that becomes one who has been thus saved from the guilt of sin and for whom salvation has been provided from the power of sin. It is at the very beginning of this great portion of the Scriptures that this practical appeal is made. The passage states: "I beseech you therefore, brethren, by the mercies of God, that ye present [the same word as 'yield,' in Romans 6:13] your bodies a living sacrifice, holy, acceptable unto God, which is your reasonable service. And be not conformed to this world: but be ye transformed [transfigured] by the renewing of your mind, that ye may prove what is that good, and acceptable, and perfect, will of God."

The words "I beseech you" are far removed from being a command. It is a pleading for that manner of life which becomes the children of God. It is not something that we *must* do to be saved: it is something we *should* do because we are saved. The first exhortation in this practical portion of this Epistle of salvation is for dedication of the whole body as a living sacrifice. This should not be called "consecration"; for consecration is an act of God. The believer may lay down, yield, or dedicate; but God must take up and apply what is presented. That is consecration. Again, there is little Scripture to warrant a supposed "*re*consecration." We cannot partly choose the will of God as the rule of our lives. We have not chosen to do His will until we have really become willing to do His will. True dedication, therefore, does not call for a *re*consecration to God. There is no mention here of some particular service that might be made an issue of willingness. It is only self-dedication to whatsoever God may choose for us, now, or ever. Such is our "reasonable service," if it is "holy and acceptable unto God." When we are not conformed to this world and when we are transfigured by the renewing of our minds, we will make full proof in our lives of "that good, and acceptable, and perfect will of God" for us. Thus yieldedness is presented as the first and all-important issue for the one that is saved. Following in this portion of the Scriptures there is much teaching about service; but even the appeal for service could be of no avail until there has been a presentation of the whole body as a living sacrifice.

CHRIST THE PATTERN

One of the human perfections of the Lord Jesus was His complete yieldedness to the will of His Father. The Scriptures bear abundant testimony to this. In Hebrews 10:5-7 we have the record: "Wherefore when he cometh into the world, he saith, Sacrifice and offering thou wouldest not, but a body hast thou prepared me: in burnt offerings and sacrifices for sin thou hast had no pleasure. Then said I, Lo, I come (in the volume of the book it is written of me), to do thy will, O God." He was yielded to His Father's will. His yieldedness included even His human body ("but a body hast thou prepared me"), the sacrifice of which was to give value to every acceptable animal sacrifice that had gone before, and to supersede any attempted sacrifice that might follow. When He was nearing His cross He said: "Nevertheless not my will, but thine, be done." Again, it is recorded of Him in Psalm 22 that He said to His Father: "But thou art holy," and this He said at the darkest hour of His crucifixion when He was crying, "My God, my God, why hast thou forsaken me?" Yet again, in Philippians 2:8, we are told that He "became obedient unto death, even the death of the cross."

The absolute yieldedness of the Son to do the Father's will is not only the supreme example of a normal attitude of a child of God toward his Father, but such an attitude is to be imparted and maintained in the believer's heart by the Spirit, after the first act of dedication has been accomplished. The following passage is an exhortation to this end: "Let this mind be in you, which was also in Christ Jesus" (Philippians 2:5). The first word of this passage is most illuminating; for in this little word "let" is compressed the whole Bible teaching concerning the believer's responsibility toward the possible manifestation of Christ in the daily life by the Spirit. We could not produce such a manifestation; but we can "let" it be done in us by Another. The issue, it is clear, is not that of resolving to *do* anything: it is rather that of an attitude of willingness that Another may do according to the last degree of His blessed will. Then, lest we might not realize the exact character of the mind of Christ which we are to "*let*" be reproduced in us and might be unprepared for the out-working of those particular elements in our daily life, an explicit and detailed description of the elements of "the mind of Christ" is recorded. These elements are fundamental: "Who, being in the form of God, thought it not robbery to be equal with God: but made himself of no reputation, and took upon him the form of a servant, and was made in the likeness of men: and being found in fashion as a man, he humbled himself, and became obedient unto death, even the death of the cross. Wherefore God also hath highly exalted him" (vs. 6-9).

It should be noted that these particulars which taken together form the "mind of Christ" are not mentioned merely to relate facts about Jesus Christ: they are presented that we may be fully aware of just what is to be reproduced in us, and just what we are to "*let*" Him do in us and through us. The divinely produced manifestation in the believer's life will be "the mind of Christ"; but this, we are assured from all Scripture, is wrought by the power of the Spirit. "For to me to live is Christ." That is an *effect*. The *cause* is the power of the Spirit of God. Out of much that the passage reveals, at least three things may be mentioned:

First, Christ was willing to *go* where His Father chose. He was at home in the glory. It was His native environment; but He came into this world with a mission and message of grace. "God had an only Son and He was a foreign missionary." Such was His Father's will for Him, and His attitude may be expressed by the familiar words: "I'll go where You want me to go, dear Lord."

Second, Christ was willing to *be* whatever His Father chose. "He made Himself of no reputation." He was not only willing to lay aside the garments of His glory, but He was willing, as well, to be set at naught, to be spit upon and to be crucified. That was the Father's will for Him and His attitude may be expressed in the words: "I'll *be* what You want me to be."

Third, Christ was willing to *do* whatever His Father chose. He became obedient unto death, and in so doing, His attitude may again be expressed in the words: "I'll *do* what You want me to do."[1]

Many sing the words of the hymn above quoted who may never have faced the question of a positive surrender to the will of God. There can be no true spirituality until this surrender is made. But when it is done, God imparts the sufficient power for the realization of all His will. This passage closes with these words: "For it is God which worketh [energizes] in you both to will and to do of his good pleasure." Thus He undertakes and continues the flow of every spiritual reality in the life that is normally adjusted to Him (Galatians 3:3).

Our Lord when dealing with this great theme of the Christian's responsibility in being wholly yielded to God, spoke of it as abiding in Him (John 15:1-17). The results of an abiding life are three-fold: (1) *Prayer is effectual:* "If ye abide in me, and my words abide in you, ye shall ask what ye will, and it shall be done unto you"; (2) *Joy is celestial:* "These things have I spoken unto you, that my joy might remain in you, and that your joy might be full"; (3) *Fruit is perpetual:* "Ye have not chosen me, but I have chosen you, and ordained you, that you should go and bring forth fruit, and that your fruit should remain." These results include all that is vital in a spiritual life and are conditioned by Christ upon obedience to all that He has said: "If ye keep my commandments, ye shall abide in my love; even as I have kept my Father's commandments, and abide in his love." Abiding, then, is simply yielding to the known will of our Lord, just as He was yielded to His Father's will.

A yieldedness to the will of God is not demonstrated by some one particular issue: it is rather a matter of having taken the will of God as the rule of one's life. To be in the will of God is simply to be willing to do His will without reference to any particular thing He may choose. It is electing His will to be final, even before we know what He may wish us to do. It is, therefore, not a question of being willing to do some one thing: it is a question of being willing to do *anything*, when, where and how, it may seem best in His heart of love. It is taking the normal

[1]See also page 94.

and natural position of childlike trust which has already con-
sented to the wish of the Father even before anything of the
outworking of His wish is revealed. This distinction cannot be
over-emphasized. It is quite natural to be saying: "If He wishes
me to do something, let Him tell me and I will then determine
what I will do." To a person in such an attitude of heart He
reveals nothing. There must be a covenant relationship of trust
in which His will is assented to *once for all* and without reserva-
tion. Why should it not be so? Might not our reluctance sometimes be stated in the words, "I know thee, hard taskmaster!"
Is *He* a hard taskmaster? Is there any hope whatsoever that
we of ourselves might be wise enough to choose what is best
if we keep the directing of our lives in our own hands? Will the
Father, whose love is infinite, impose upon His child? Or will
He ever be careless?

We make no promise that we will not sin or violate the will
of God when we yield to Him. We do not promise to change
our own desires. The exact human attitude has been expressed
in the words: "I am willing to be made willing to do His will."
Let it be stated again that this question, so simple in itself,
instantly becomes complicated when related to any concrete
issue of obedience. It is the question only of the will of God in
the abstract in which we have the assurance that in every detail
He will work in us that which is well pleasing in His sight. He
will work in us both to will and to do of His good pleasure.

We may experience long waiting to ascertain what His will
may be; but when it is clearly revealed, there can be no room
for debate in the heart that would not quench the Spirit.

KNOWING THE WILL OF GOD

There is often a desire to understand more fully just how we
may know the will of God. To this it may be answered:

First, His leading is only for those who are already committed
to do as He may choose. To such it may be said: "God is able
to speak loud enough to make a *willing* soul hear."

Second, The divine leading will always be according to the
Scriptures. To His Word we may always go with prayerful

expectation; yet it is most perilous to treat the Bible as a magic lottery. We do not learn the meaning of a passage by "casting lots." We do not find out the will of God from the Bible by opening the Book and abiding by the sentiment of the first verse we may chance to read. It is not a matter of chance, nor is our relation to His Word so superficial that we may expect to find His blessed mind for us by blindly reading one chance verse. We are to study and know the Scriptures that every word of His testimony may instruct us.

Third, He does not lead His children by any *rules* whatsoever. No two of His children will be led alike and it is most probable that He will never lead any one of His children twice in exactly the same way. Therefore rules are apt to be misleading. True spirituality consists in a life which is free from law and which is lived, to the minutest detail of individuality, by the power of the Spirit.

Fourth, The divine leading is by the Spirit who *indwells* the Christian. It follows, therefore, that true leading, in this dispensation, will be more by an inner consciousness than by outward signs. After we have faithfully met the conditions for a spiritual life, we have "the mind of the Spirit." He is both able to convince us of what is wrong and to impart a clear conviction as to what is right. Because of our present unique relation to the Spirit, it is hardly necessary, or wise, to depend much on "fleeces" or a "pillar of cloud"; though sometimes He may lead through these external things. It is God which worketh *in* you both to will and to do of His good pleasure. We must learn the reality of the indwelling Spirit and what it means to "walk" in Him.

To be guided by the Spirit is to be moved through the most delicate relationships the heart can know. The "bit and bridle" must give way to the glance of the eye (Psalm 32:8, 9). At this point Satan, appearing as "an angel of light," will seek to confuse the mind by presenting his counterfeits of the leading of God. Every Christian should be aware of this danger. To misdirect the believer's life, Satan makes use of a morbid conscience, a mistaken impression as to duty, or a lack of understanding as to the exact teachings of God's Word. However Satan's leadings are to be detected since they are irksome, painful, and disagreeable. The leading of the Spirit is sweet and satisfying to the heart of the one who is yielded to God. We must remember that the will of God is said to be "good," "acceptable," and "perfect" (Romans 12:2), and that when we are walking with Him, He works in us "both to will and to do of his good pleasure" (Philippians 2:13). He it is Who is working in us "that which is wellpleasing in his sight" (Hebrews 13:21).

On the divine side, the yielding of the human will is seen to be imperative. The Father cannot suffer rebellion in His household, nor can He realize His blessed designs for His child until His judgment is freely acknowledged to be best. There is a distinction to be noted between chastisement for correction, which may often be repeated, and the once for all "scourging" which *every* son must receive (Hebrews 12:6) One is unto correction as often as it is needed; but the other is the once for all conquering of the human will. When our will is thus conquered, it does not follow that our will is weakened in relationships with our fellow men. The will has been yielded to *God*. How simple all this might be; yet what years of scourging many have suffered only because they would not be normal in relation to the mind of God for them! Not all affliction is to be counted as scourging. When it is scourging, we shall be conscious of our own stubbornness in not yielding. There need be no uncertainty concerning this matter.

Yielding to the mind and will of God is a definite act which opens the gate into the divinely appointed path, wherein we may walk in all fellowship and service with Christ. A child of God cannot consider himself to be in the appointed path if, within the range of his understanding of himself, he has no consciousness that he is subject to the will of God. "I came not to do my own will, but the will of him that sent me" was the pattern of yieldedness as revealed in Christ. It is recorded of Christ in Psalm 40:6 that He said to His Father: "Mine ears hast thou opened" (lit. bored). This is doubtless a reference to the law of the bond-servant who, having been set free, yielded himself to his master forever (Exodus 21:5, 6). "And that he died for all, that they which live should not henceforth live unto themselves, but unto him which died for them, and rose again" (II Corinthians 5:15).

WHAT IS A SACRIFICIAL LIFE?

The highest motive for yielding to the will of God is not the mere desire for victory in life, or for power, or blessing. It is that we may live the sacrificial life which is the Christ life. Sacrificial does not mean *painful;* it is simply doing Another's will. Some pain may be in the path; but the prevailing note is *joy,* and the blessing of the heart is *peace*.

Every child of God, then, must definitely yield to the will of God. Not concerning some one issue of the daily life; but as an abiding attitude toward God. Apart from that there can be no true spirituality and no escape from the Father's scourging hand; for He cannot, and will not, suffer His child to live on without the priceless blessings that His love is longing to bestow. Satan's sin against God in the primal glory was a five-fold expression of the two defiant words: "*I will*" (Isaiah 14:13, 14), and every unyielded life is perpetuating the crime of Satan. To be spiritual we must not say "*no*" to God. "Quench not the Spirit."

CHAPTER 6

"WALK IN THE SPIRIT"

THE THIRD CONDITION OF TRUE SPIRITUALITY

TRUE SPIRITUALITY also depends upon a positive attitude of *reliance* upon the presence and power of the indwelling Spirit. The two previously mentioned conditions have been negative in character. They represent things the believer, to be spiritual, must *not* do. He must *not* grieve the Spirit by retaining unconfessed any known sin. He must *not* quench the Spirit by saying "no" to God. The third, and last, condition is positive in character. It is something the believer, to be spiritual, must *do*.

WHAT IS MEANT BY "WALK IN THE SPIRIT"?

There are several passages of Scripture in which this vital issue appears; but it is, perhaps most directly stated in Galatians 5:16: "This I say then, Walk in the Spirit, and ye shall not fulfil the lust of the flesh." The passage is better rendered: "This I say then, By means of the Spirit be walking, and ye shall not fulfil the lust of the flesh." The child of God has no power within himself whereby he can enter, promote, or maintain a "walk in the Spirit." This Scripture, when rightly rendered, does not make the impossible demand upon a Christian that he, in his own strength, is to accomplish a "walk in the Spirit." It is rather revealed that the Spirit will do the walking in the Christian. The human responsibility is that of a whole dependence upon the Spirit. Walking by means of the Spirit is simply walking by a definite reliance upon the ability and power of the One who indwells. The same truth, though differently presented, is stated in verse 18: "But if ye be led of the Spirit, ye are not under the law." In no sense does the believer lead, or direct, the Spirit. He can, however, be dependent on the Spirit, and this is his exact responsibility as revealed in this passage.

The third condition of true spirituality is, then, an unbroken reliance upon the Spirit to do what He has come to do and what He alone can do. Such is the Father's provision that sin may be *prevented* in the life of His child. The results of the outworking of this divine provision are beyond our powers of estimation: "Ye shall not fulfil the lust of the flesh."

It is often the "beginning of days" in a Christian's life when he really believes and heeds the Word of God enough to be made aware of his own limitations, and seriously considers the exact revelation as to what he of himself can or cannot do, and what the Spirit who indwells him has come to do. We seldom attempt to do the work we have engaged another to do. We naturally *rely* on the person we have engaged to do it. Have we ever learned to *depend* on the Spirit for anything? Are we intelligently counting on the Spirit to undertake those particular things which, according to the Scriptures, He is appointed to do? Do we really believe we are just as helpless as His Word declares us to be? Do we really believe He is able and waiting to do every thing we cannot do? Having begun in the Spirit, so far as the divine undertaking in salvation is concerned, are we now to be perfected by the flesh? In meeting the impossible issues of a true Christian life, are we consciously living upon a *works*-principle, or upon a *faith*-principle? The Bible emphatically declares the believer to be upon a *faith-principle* when he is really within the plan of God for his daily life. These uncomplicated teachings are on the pages of God's Book and an attentive Christian can hardly avoid them.

The God-honoring quality of life is always the divine objective in the believer's daily life. Its realization is never by a human resolution or struggle or the resources of the flesh: it is by "fighting the good fight of faith." There is a wide difference between "fighting" to do w h a t G o d a l o n e c a n d o, and "fighting" to maintain an attitude of dependence on Him to do what He alone can do. The child of God has an all-engaging responsibility of *continuing* in an attitude of reliance upon the Spirit. This is the point of his constant attention. This is his divinely appointed task and place of co-operation in the mighty undertakings of God. The locomotive engineer will accomplish little when pushing his ponderous train. He is not appointed to such a service. His real usefulness will begin when he takes his place at the throttle. The important conflict in the believer's life is to *maintain* the unbroken attitude of reliance upon the Spirit. Thus, and only thus, can the Spirit possess and vitalize every human faculty, emotion and choice.

It is in every sense the Christian's own life which is lived and his only consciousness will be that of the use of his own faculties: but all these will be empowered by the Spirit as they otherwise could not be. The empowering work of the Spirit does not set aside the normal functions of the human soul and spirit. He works *through* unto fulness of power which realizes the blessed will of God. "If by means of the Spirit ye are walking, ye shall not fulfil the lust of the flesh." "Faith is the victory that overcomes the world."

Rationalism is directly opposed to faith. There are those who rebel at the teaching that salvation is by faith alone. They rebel either because they do not know, or do not believe, the Word of God. There are those, likewise, who rebel at the teaching that an unbroken victory in the believer's daily life is by faith alone, and this, too, is either because they do not know, or do not believe, the Scriptures. The doctrine concerning a divinely produced sanctity of life does not rest upon one or two proof texts. It is one of the great themes, if not the most extensive, theme in the Epistles; for not only is the doctrine taught at length, but every injunction to the Christian is based upon the exact principles revealed in the doctrine. It is one of the most vital elements in the age-characterizing provisions in grace.

THREE REASONS FOR RELIANCE UPON THE SPIRIT

The Bible assigns at least three outstanding causes which hinder spirituality in the child of God, making necessary implicit and constant reliance upon the indwelling Spirit: (1) "The world," or the opposite of the heavenly standards; (2) "The flesh," or that within the Christian which opposes the Spirit by "lusting" against the Spirit; and (3) "The devil," who opposes every plan and purpose of God. These are now to be taken up more at length, but in a different order:

First, The Impossible Heavenly Standard of Life in Contrast to the Standards of the World

God has but one Book and that Book includes all people of every dispensation. In it we find His will and purpose for Israel in the age before the cross, and His will and purpose for Israel and all the Gentile nations in the age to come. So, also, we find His will and purpose for the heavenly people of the present dispensation. The children of Israel were redeemed and delivered out of Egypt and He gave to them their rule of life which should govern them in their land. These particular rules were never addressed to any other people than Israel, and these rules addressed to Israel made their appeal to the "natural man." They ceased to be in effect, as the required rule of life, after the death of Christ (John 1:17; Romans 6:14; II Corinthians 3:1-13; Galatians 5:18). There is also revealed a rule of life which is to govern Israel when she is regathered and reestablished in her own land under the earth-wide rule of her Messiah King. His reign will be legal in character, or of the character of the law. Its principles are stated and anticipated by the prophets of the Old Testament and are also further revealed by passages in the New Testament. The Bible also contains a rule of life which applies to the heavenly citizens of the present dispensation, who, though heavenly in position and responsibility, are called upon to live as "pilgrims and strangers" in the earth, and as witnesses in the enemy's land. Their governing principles will be found stated in The Acts and the Epistles and portions of the Gospels. These heavenly standards are not imposed upon the unregenerate world. They have not received the Spirit and therefore have no enablement whereby they might live according to the standards which are committed to the Christian. It is both useless and unreasonable to apply Christian standards to an unregenerate world. Again, the heavenly standard of life is as much higher in character than Israel's law, as heavenly citizenship is higher than a citizenship in the earth. Israel's law incorporated many of the eternal principles growing out of the very character of God. These principles, as such, do not pass away; but the exact manner of their statement is changed that they may be adapted to the new relationships which the heavenly people sustain to God. Thus the believer is "not under the law"; though nine commandments of Moses in the Decalogue are carried forward and reappear with a different character and emphasis within the injunctions under grace. Neither is he "without law," being inlawed to Christ. There is priceless value in knowing all that God has spoken to any people at any time; but the Christian is primarily concerned with the exact purpose and plan of God for him. The heavenly citizen will not find the full revelation of the will of God for him in any portion of the Scriptures spoken to people of other ages; though he may find much that is in common. There can be no clear apprehension of God's Book apart from this distinction.

In the Scriptures the Christian is addressed as a supernatural man and a superhuman manner of life is placed before him. This is reasonable. Christians are citizens of heaven from the moment they are saved and it is naturally required of them that they "walk worthy of their heavenly calling." From such a consistent life they cannot be excused. They are not made citizens by any manner of life, but being made citizens by the power of God, it becomes them to *live* according to the position that God has given them.

The following passages will serve to illustrate the superhuman character of the present rule of life for the child of God under grace:

"A new commandment I give unto you, That ye love one another; as I have loved you, that ye also love one another" (John 13:34); "This is my commandment, that ye love one another, as I have loved you" (John 15:12). The *law* required love to be to another "as thyself." To love *as* Christ has loved us is infinitely higher, and humanly impossible.

"And grieve not the Holy Spirit of God" (Ephesians 4:30).

"And bringing into captivity every thought to the obedience of Christ" (II Corinthians 10:5).

"Giving thanks always for all things unto God and the Father in the name of our Lord Jesus Christ" (Ephesians 5:20).

"That ye should shew forth the praises [virtues] of him who hath called you out of darkness into his marvellous light" (I Peter 2:9).

"Rejoice evermore, Pray without ceasing" (I Thessalonians 5:16, 17).

"I therefore, the prisoner of the Lord, beseech you that ye walk worthy of the vocation wherewith ye are called. With all lowliness and meekness, with longsuffering, forbearing one another in love; endeavoring to keep the unity of the Spirit in the bond of peace" (Ephesians 4:1-3).

Though these passages present impossible demands upon the human resource, God most evidently expects them to be realized in every believer's daily life. He knows better than we that we could never produce any such quality of life; yet He is not unreasonable in His expectation, since He stands ready to supply *all* that He demands. The Spirit indwells the believer for this very purpose. Of our own selves, we are not asked even to attempt these standards. The Epistles are full of assurances that the imparted energy of God through the Spirit is sufficient for all that God has required. "It is God which worketh [energizes] in you both to will and to do of his good pleasure."

The new rule of life which is placed before the child of God under grace is, then, impossible from the human standpoint, and its realization must depend on a definite reliance upon the indwelling Spirit to do the whole will of God. A Christian, to be spiritual, must "walk by means of the Spirit."

SECOND, THE CHRISTIAN FACES A WORLD-RULING FOE

The Bible represents Satan as the enemy of the saints of God and especially is this seen to be true of the saints of this age. There is no controversy between Satan and unsaved people; for they are a part of his world-system. They have not been deliv-

ered from the powers of darkness and translated into the kingdom of the Son of God. Satan is the energizing power in those
who are unsaved (Ephesians 2:2), as God is the energizing
power in those who are saved (Philippians 2:13). Every human
being is either under the power of Satan, or under the power of
God. This is not to say that Christians may not be influenced
by Satan and the unsaved not influenced by the Spirit of
God; but their position is in one domain or the other, and Satan's
domain is not in all matters characterized by things that are
inherently evil as those things are estimated by the world. Satan's
life-purpose is to be "like the Most High" (Isaiah 14:14), and
he appears "as an angel of light," and his ministers "as the ministers of righteousness" (II Corinthians 11:13-15). His ministers,
being ministers of *righteousness*, preach a gospel of reformation
and salvation by human character, rather than salvation by
grace alone, unrelated to any human virtue. Therefore the world,
with all its moral standards and culture, is not necessarily free
from the power and energizing control of Satan. He would promote forms of religion and human excellence apart from the
redemption that is in Christ, and the world is evidently energized to undertake that very thing. He has blinded the unsaved;
but concerning one thing only: they are blinded by Satan lest
the light of the gospel should shine unto them (II Corinthians
4:3, 4).

The enmity of Satan has always been against the Person of
God alone, and not against humanity. It is only when we have
"partaken of the divine nature" that we are possessed with a new
and mighty foe. The thrusts of his "fiery darts" are aimed at God
who indwells us. However, the conflict is real and the foe is
superhuman. "Finally, my brethren, be strong in the Lord, and
in the power of his might. Put on the whole armour of God, that
ye may be able to stand against the wiles [strategies] of the
devil. For we wrestle not against flesh and blood, but against
principalities, against powers, against rulers of the darkness of
this world, against spiritual wickedness in high places" (Ephesians 6:10 - 12). These world-rulers of the darkness of this age,
the spiritual powers of wickedness, who are here said to wage

a ceaseless conflict against us, cannot be overcome by human strategy or strength. The Bible lends no sanction to foolish suppositions that the devil will flee at the mere resistance of a determined human will. We are to "resist the devil," but it must be done "steadfast in the faith," and while "submitting" ourselves unto God (James 4:7; I Peter 5:9). Satan, being by creation superior to all other creatures cannot be conquered by one of them. Even Michael the archangel, we are told, "when contending with the devil . . . durst not bring against him a railing accusation, but said, The Lord rebuke thee." Michael the archangel does not contend with Satan. He must depend on the power of Another; thus acting on a principle of *faith*, rather than on a principle of *works*. Certainly a Christian, with all his limitations, must appeal to the power of God in the conflict with this mighty foe, and he is directed to do this: "Above all, taking the shield of faith, wherewith ye shall be able to quench all the fiery darts of the wicked [one]" (Ephesians 6:16).[1]

The believer's conflict with Satan is as fierce and unceasing as that mighty being can make it. Before him we of ourselves are as nothing; but God has anticipated our helplessness and provided a perfect victory through the indwelling Spirit: "Because greater is he that is in you, than he that is in the world" (I John 4:4). A Christian, because of the power of the new enemy, must "walk by means of the Spirit" if he would be spiritual.

Third, The Adamic Nature

Careless Christians are not concerned with the Person and work of the Holy Spirit, or with the exact distinctions which condition true spirituality; but these distinctions and conditions do appeal to those who really desire a life that is well pleasing to God. We find that Satan has pitfalls and counterfeit doctrines in the realm of the deepest spiritual realities. The majority of these false teachings are based on a misapprehension of the Bible teaching about *sin*, especially the sin question as related to the believer.

---

[1]A more extended treatment of the Bible teachings on this subject will be found in the author's book "Satan."

The Scripture is "profitable for doctrine, for reproof, for correction, for instruction in righteousness: that the man of God may be perfect [full grown], throughly furnished unto all good works" (II Timothy 3:16, 17); but in the same Epistle we are also urged to "study" and "rightly divide" the Word of Truth. It should be noted that two out of four of the values of the Scriptures in the life of the "man of God," as recorded in the above passage are *"reproof"* and *"correction"*; yet how few, especially of those who are holding an error, are of a teachable spirit. It seems to be one of the characteristics of all Satanic errors that those who have embraced them seem never inclined honestly to reconsider their ground. They read only their sectarian, or misleading literature and often carefully avoid hearing any corrective teaching from the Word of God. This difficulty is greatly increased when their error has led them to assume some unwarranted position regarding a supposed deliverance from sin, or personal attainments in holiness. A *"correction,"* or *"reproof,"* to such seems to be a suggestion toward "backsliding," and no zealously minded person will easily choose such a course. Much error is thriving along these lines with no other dynamic than human zeal, and the Word of God is persistently distorted to maintain human theories. Many of these errors are reproved and corrected when the fundamental distinction is recognized between the Christian's *position* in Christ and his *experience* in daily life. Whatever God has done for us in Christ is perfect and complete; but such perfection should not be confused with the imperfect daily life.

There are five Biblical doctrines which are closely related to the question of sin in the believer which are most commonly misunderstood, and which, if perverted, may be used of the enemy to drive even serious minded believers into most misleading presumption and harmful error. These doctrines are: (1) The fact of the continued presence of the Adamic nature in the believer, which is the present theme; (2) The divine cure for the effects of sin in the spiritual life of a Christian, already considered; (3) The Bible teaching about perfection; (4) The Bible teaching about sanctification; and, (5) the Bible teaching about the believer's death in Christ. That there may be a clearer understanding of the present theme, the Bible teaching about perfection and sanctification are first to be considered briefly. The Bible teaching about the believer's death in Christ will be taken up at a later and more appropriate point in this discussion.

THE DOCTRINE OF PERFECTION

In the Word of God, perfection is presented in seven aspects:

(1) *The Old Testament use of the word as applied to persons.*

The word in the Old Testament has the meaning of "sincere" and "upright." Noah was "perfect" (Genesis 6:9); Job was "perfect" (Job 1:1, 8); In avoiding the sins of the nations, Israel might be "perfect" (Deuteronomy 18:13); The end of the "perfect" man was peace (Psalm 37:37); So, also, the saints of the Old Testament order will appear in heaven as "the spirits of just men made perfect" (Hebrews 12:23). The Bible does not teach that these people were *sinless.*

(2) *Positional perfection in Christ.*

"For by one offering he hath perfected for ever them that are sanctified" (Hebrews 10:14). This is clearly the perfection of the work of Christ for us and must not be related to the Christian's daily life.

(3) *Spiritual maturity and understanding.*

"Howbeit we speak wisdom among them that are perfect" (full grown, I Corinthians 2:6, cf. 14:20. See, also, II Corinthians 13:11; Philippians 3:15; II Timothy 3:17).

(4) *Perfection which is progressive.*

"Are ye so foolish? having begun in the Spirit, are ye now made [to be made] perfect by the flesh?" (Galatians 3:3).

(5) *Perfection in some one particular.*

(a) In the will of God: "That ye stand perfect and complete in all the will of God" (Colossians 4:12).

(b) In imitating one aspect of the goodness of God: "Be ye therefore perfect, even as your Father which is in heaven is perfect" (Matthew 5:48). The context is of the Father's love for His enemies and the injunction is that this aspect of the Father's goodness should be reproduced.

(c) In service: "Make you perfect in every good work" (Hebrews 13:21).

(d) In patience: "But let patience have her perfect work, that ye may be perfect [mature] and entire, wanting nothing" (James 1:4).

(6) *The ultimate perfection of the individual in heaven.*

"Whom we preach, warning every man, and teaching every man in all wisdom; that we may present every man perfect in Christ" (Colossians 1:28, cf. Colossians 1:22; Philippians 3:12; I Peter 5:10; I Thessalonians 3:13).

(7) *The ultimate perfection of the corporate body of believers in heaven.*

"Till we all come in the unity of the faith, and of the knowledge of the Son of God, unto a perfect man, unto the measure of the stature of the fulness of Christ" (Ephesians 4:13. See also, 5:27; John 17:23; Jude 24; Revelation 14:5).

The word "perfection" as found in the New Testament is a translation from either one of two Greek words, one meaning "mature" and the other meaning "adjusted." And it is obvious that neither of these words etymologically considered has any reference to sinlessness. These facts should be estimated most carefully by any who have attempted the formation of a doctrine on the somewhat misleading use of the English word "perfect." At this very point we may possibly discover the Scriptures to be unto us a word of "reproof" or "correction." There is a complete deliverance by the Spirit for every child of God, but this should not be confused with any use of the word "perfect" when the incapacity to sin is implied by the use of that word.

THE DOCTRINE OF SANCTIFICATION

Again the doctrine must not be made to exceed that which is actually expressed by the Biblical use of the word "sanctify." To discover the full scope and meaning of this word it is necessary to include all passages in the Old and New Testament wherein it is used and to add to these as well all passages wherein the words "saint" and "holy" are used, since these three words are translations, both from the Hebrew and from the Greek, of the same root word.

The root meaning of "sanctify," "saint" and "holy" is that a person or thing is thereby said to be set apart, or classified; usually as pertaining unto God.

Though these words and the truth they express are found throughout the whole Bible, this discussion is concerned only with that aspect of the teaching which applies to the child of God under grace.[1] Here we find that believers are the objects of a three-fold sanctification:

First, Positional sanctification

"But of him are ye in Christ Jesus, who of God is made unto us . . . sanctification" (I Corinthians 1:30); "By the which will we are sanctified through the offering of the body of Jesus Christ once for all" (Hebrews 10:10). Thus, also, the Apostle addresses *all* believers as "saints," and in the Scriptures reference is made to "holy prophets," "holy brethren," "holy priests," "holy women," "holy nation." Such they are by their *position* in Christ. He even addressed the Corinthian believers as "saints" and as already "sanctified" (I Corinthians 1:2; 6:11); yet this very letter was written to correct those Christians because of terrible sin (I Corinthians 5:1, 2; 6:1, 7, 8). They were "saints" and "sanctified" *in Christ*, but were far from being such in daily life.

Second, Experimental sanctification

This aspect of the work of God for the believer is *progressive* in some of its aspects, and is quite in contrast to the *positional* sanctification which is "once for all." It is accomplished by the power of God through the Spirit and through the Word: "Sanctify them through thy truth: thy word is truth" (John 17:17. See, also, II Corinthians 3:18; Ephesians 5:25, 26; I Thessalonians 5:23; II Peter 3:18).

---

[1]This subject is treated more fully in a pamphlet by the author entitled, "Sanctification."

Experimental sanctification is according to various relationships.

(1) In relation to the believer's yieldedness to God.

By presenting his body a living sacrifice, the child of God thereby is set apart unto God and so is experimentally sanctified. The presentation may be absolute and thus admit of no progression, or it may be partial and so require a further development. In either case it is experimental sanctification.

(2) In relation to sin.

The child of God may so comply with every condition for true spirituality as to be experiencing *all* the provided deliverance and victory from the power of sin, or, on the other hand, he may be experiencing a partial deliverance from the power of sin. In either case he is set apart and is thus experimentally sanctified.

(3) In relation to Christian growth.

This aspect of experimental sanctification in every case is progressive. It should in no way be confused with incomplete yieldedness to God or incomplete victory over sin. Its meaning is that the knowledge of truth, devotion and experience are naturally subject to development. By virtue of their present development, as Christians, believers experimentally are set apart unto God. That development should be advanced with each passing day. And thus, again, the Christian is subject to an experimental sanctification which is progressive.

Third, Ultimate sanctification.

Even *experimental* sanctification will be perfected when the saints are gathered into His presence in glory. "When he shall appear, we shall be like him," and "conformed to the image of his Son" (John 3:2; Romans 8:29).

The Bible teaching in regard to sanctification, then, is (1) that *all* believers are *positionally* sanctified in Christ "once for all" at the moment they are saved. This sanctification is as perfect as He is perfect. (2) All believers are *being* sanctified by the power of God through the Word and this sanctification is as perfect as the *believer* is perfect. So, also, (3) all believers *will be* sanctified and perfected in the glory into the very image of the Son of God. The Bible, therefore, does not teach that any child of God is wholly sanctified in daily life before that final consummation of all things.

THE DOCTRINE OF THE ADAMIC NATURE

The third and last reason to be mentioned as to why the believer must consciously rely on the Spirit, as has been stated, is that he still possesses the Adamic nature over which he, of himself, has no sufficient control. The Christian is saved and safe in the grace of God; but he cannot command himself into a God-honoring manner of life. For this he must rely upon divine power in order that he may be saved from the *power* of sin, as he has already relied on the power of God to save him from the *penalty* of sin. Salvation into safety, or sanctity, is all a work of God *in* and *for* the one who trusts Him.

The fact that the unregenerate possess a fallen nature is generally admitted. The misunderstanding is with regard to the Christian. The Bible teaching is clear, and yet some professing Christians are misled into assuming that they do not any longer possess the tendency to sin.[1] This question may be discussed both from the experimental and from the Biblical standpoint.

Experimentally, the most saintly of God's children have been conscious of the presence and power of a fallen nature. This may be called the normal consciousness of the devout believer. Such a consciousness is not an evidence of immaturity: it is rather the evidence of true humility and clear vision of one's own heart. It does not imply a lack of fellowship with God occasioned by a grieving of the Holy Spirit through sin. Who can hate sin more than the one who is *aware* of its presence and power? And who is in greater danger of its havoc in his spiritual life than the one who in unwarranted presumption has assumed that the disposition to sin has been removed? The contention that one has no disposition to sin must be based upon a shocking

---

[1]See also page 138.

lack of self-knowledge as to the motives and impulses of the heart, or such an assumption is made through failure to comprehend the true character of sin itself. If an individual can convince himself that sin is something different from *anything* he ever does, or is inclined to do; beyond *anything* he ever thinks, feels or undertakes, he can doubtless convince himself that he has not sinned. If, in his own mind, one can modify the character of sin, he can, by that process, relieve himself from the *consciousness* of sin. There are not a few such people in the world today. Truth can not stand when based upon a human experience. It must be based upon revelation.

Sin is not what some prejudiced, misguided person *claims* it to be: it is what God has *revealed* it to be. Sin has been well defined, from a study of the whole testimony of the Word of God, to be "any violation of, or want of conformity to, the revealed will of God." It is "missing the mark." But what mark? Surely the *divine* standard. Have we done *all* and *only* His will with motives as pure as heaven and in the unchanging faithfulness of the Infinite? God has provided a perfect victory; but we have all often failed in its realization. If possessed with any degree of the knowledge of God and self-knowledge, we are aware that we are too often far from *sinless* in the eyes of God. The consciousness of sinfulness at times has been the testimony of the most spiritual believers of all generations as they have been enabled to see the Person of God. Job, the upright in heart, abhorred himself before God. Daniel, against whom no sin is recorded, said, "My comeliness was turned in me into corruption."

In considering the Biblical testimony concerning the sins of the Christian two questions may reasonably be asked: (1) "From what source does sin proceed in the child of God?" and, (2) "What is the divine remedy?" There is abundant answer to these questions in the Word of God.

I. FROM WHAT SOURCE DOES SIN PROCEED IN A CHRISTIAN?

Sin is the fruit of a fallen nature. This has always been so, with the exception of the first sin which resulted in the fall. We sin *because* of a fallen nature received from Adam, and from countless generations of sinning parents. This is true of the unregenerate: it is equally true of the regenerate. Yet it is claimed by some that a Christian who is supposed to have been delivered from the sin nature, can still *continue* sinning as Adam sinned, — from an unfallen nature. Adam sinned but once from an unfallen nature, and no one else has so sinned from that time until now. Could we now be placed in the same state as our first parents, we would not be able to sin and still *maintain* that position. The first sin we committed would result in our return to a fallen state. Where would such a person be spiritually after he has sinned, if the experience of Adam is of any value as evidence in the case?

The Bible teaching on the subject of the Christian's sin may be better understood if three important words are defined:

"FLESH" (Gr. sarx)

The word, in its general use, refers to the physical body. It however has a moral, or ethical, meaning as well and with this we are concerned. "Flesh," when used in the Bible with a moral meaning, refers to more than the physical body; it includes in its meaning the whole of the unregenerate person, — spirit, soul and body. It includes the body, but it also includes the human spirit and soul as animating the body. A physical body is "flesh" whether dead or alive. But the moral use of the word implies that it is alive and includes that which makes it alive and that which expresses itself through the physical body. The life impulses and desires are called "lusts of the flesh." "If by the Spirit ye are walking, ye shall not fulfil the lust of the flesh" (Galatians 5:16. See also, Ephesians 2:3; II Peter 2:18; I John 2:16; Romans 13:14). That the Bible use of the word "lust" is not limited to inordinate desires is evidenced by the fact that the Holy Spirit is said to "lust against the flesh," according to the next verse in this context (see, also, James 4:5). The Scriptures are still more explicit concerning the breadth of the meaning of this word. Reference is made to "fleshly wisdom" (II Corinthians 1:12); "fleshly tables of the heart" (II Corinthians 3:3); "fleshly mind" (Colossians 2:18, cf. Romans 8:6). The Apostle does not say that either his body or nature are "fleshly"; he says, "*I* am fleshly" (Romans 7:14), and, "in *me* (that is, in my flesh), dwelleth no good thing" (Romans 7:18). "Flesh" is *self*. The unregenerate self is, within itself, hopelessly evil and condemned; but it is subject to the mighty re-creation and ultimate transformation provided for in the grace and power of God.

Into this whole "natural man" a new divine nature is imparted when we are saved. Salvation is more than a "change of heart." It is more than a transformation of the old: it is a regeneration, or creation, of something wholly new which is possessed in conjunction with the old nature so long as we are in this body. The presence of two opposing natures (not two personalities) in one individual results in conflict. "The flesh lusteth against the Spirit, and the Spirit against the flesh: and these are contrary the one to the other" (Galatians 5:17). There is no hint that this divine restraint upon the flesh will ever be unnecessary so long as we are in this body; but there is clear Bible testimony that the believer may experience an unbroken "walk in the Spirit," and "not fulfil the lust of the flesh." To secure all of this, no removal of the "flesh" is promised. The human spirit, soul and body abide, and the victory is gained over the "flesh" by the power of the indwelling Spirit.

"OLD MAN" (Gr. palaios anthropos)

This term is used only three times in the New Testament. Once it has to do with the present *position* of the "old man" through the death of Christ (Romans 6:6). In the other two passages (Ephesians 4:22-24; Colossians 3:3, 9) the fact that the "old man" has been put off for ever is made the basis of an appeal for a holy life.

In Romans 6:6 we read: "Knowing this, that our old man is [was] crucified with him." There can be no reference here to the *experience* of the Christian: it is rather a co-crucifixion "with him" and most evidently at the time and place where He was crucified.[1] In the context this passage follows immediately upon the statement concerning our transfer in federal headship from

---

[1]See also page 119-128.

the first Adam to the Last Adam (Romans 5:12-21). The first
Adam, as perpetuated in us, was judged in the crucifixion of
Christ. Our "old man," the fallen nature received from Adam,
was "crucified with him." This co-crucifixion, it will be seen, is
of the greatest importance, on the divine side, in making possible
a true deliverance from the power of the "old man." A righteous
judgment must be gained against the sin nature before any
divine work can be undertaken toward our deliverance. The
judgment is now secured, and the way is open for blessed victory
through the Spirit.

In the second passage in which the term "old man" is used,
the fact that the old man is already crucified with Christ is the
basis for an appeal: "That ye [did] put off concerning the former
conversation the old man, which is corrupt according to the
deceitful lusts; and be renewed in the spirit of your mind; and
that ye [did] put on the new man, which after God is created
in righteousness and true holiness" (Ephesians 4:22-24).

In the third passage the position suggests again the corresponding experience. "Lie not one to another, seeing that ye have
put off the old man with his deeds; and have put on the new
man, which is renewed in knowledge after the image of him that
created him" (Colossians 3:9, 10). *Positionally*, the "old man"
has been put off for ever. *Experimentally*, the "old man"
remains as an active force in the life which can be controlled
only by the power of God. We avail ourselves of that divine
sufficiency when we renounce entirely the thought of compromise
with, or toleration of, the fruit of the old nature and by faith
apply the divinely provided counter-agency for victory through
the Spirit. The result of so "reckoning" and "mortifying our
members" will be to make way for the Spirit to work out in the
life the manifestations of the "new man," Christ Jesus.[1] We
could not judge the "old man." That has been done *for* us by
Christ. Nor can we control the "old man." That is to be done *for*
us by the Spirit. "Put ye on the Lord Jesus Christ, and make not
provision for the flesh, to fulfil the lusts thereof" (Romans
13:14). The fruit of the "old man" and the fruit of the "new

---

[1]See also page 44.

man," it will be remembered, are clearly contrasted in Galatians
5:19-23: "Now the works of the flesh are manifest, which are
these; Adultery, fornication, uncleanness, lasciviousness, idolatry,
witchcraft, hatred, variance, emulations, wrath, strife, seditions,
heresies, envyings, murders, drunkenness, revellings, and such
like. . . . But the fruit of the Spirit is love, joy, peace, longsuffering, gentleness, goodness, faith, meekness, temperance"
(self-control).

There is no Biblical ground for a distinction between the
Adamic nature and a "human nature." The unregenerate have
but one nature, while the regenerate have two. There is but
one fallen nature, which is from Adam, and one new nature,
which is from God.

The "old man," then, is the Adamic nature which has been
judged in the death of Christ. It still abides with us as an
active principle in our lives, and our *experimental* victory over it
will be realized only through a definite reliance upon the indwelling Spirit. The "old man" is a part, then, but not all, of the
"flesh."

"SIN" (Gr. hamartia)

The third Bible word related to the *source* of evil in the child
of God is "sin." In certain portions of the Scriptures, notably
Romans 6:1 to 8:13 and I John 1:1 to 2:2, there is an important
distinction between two uses of the word "sin." The two meanings will be obvious if it is remembered that the word sometimes
refers to the Adamic nature, and sometimes to evil resulting from
that nature. Sin, as a nature, is the *source* of sin which is committed. Sin is the root which bears its own fruit in sin which is
evil conduct. Sin is the "old man," while sins are the manifestations in the life. Sin is what we *are* by birth, while sins are the
evil we *do* in life.

There is abundant Biblical testimony to the fact that the
"flesh," the "old man," or "sin," are the sources of evil, and are
the possession of the child of God so long as he remains in this
earthly body. He has a blessed "treasure" in the possession of
the "new man" indwelling him; but he has this treasure "in an

earthen vessel." The earthen vessel is the "body of our humiliation" (II Corinthians 4:7; Philippians 3:21).

Personality — the Ego — remains the same individuality through all the operations of grace, though it experiences the greatest possible advancement, transformation and regeneration from its lost estate in Adam, to the positions and possessions of a son of God in Christ. That which was, is said to be forgiven, justified, saved, and receives the new divine nature which is eternal life. That which was, is born again and becomes a new creature in Christ Jesus, though it remains the same personality which was born of certain parents after the flesh. Though born of God and possessing a new divine nature, the weakness of the flesh and the dispositions of the sin-nature abide until the final change from earth to heaven.

In I John 1:8, 10 we have clear warning against any presumption concerning sin. First, Christians are warned against saying that they have no sin nature: "If we say that we have no sin, we deceive ourselves, and the truth is not in us." This is distinctly concerning the sin nature of the Christian and has no application whatever to the unsaved. It is addressed to believers, and to *all* believers. It will not do to suppose that reference is made in the passage to some unfortunate, unenlightened, or unsanctified class of Christians. There is no class distinction here. It is the testimony of the Spirit of God with reference to *every* born-again person. For any such to say that he has no sin nature means that the person is self-deceived and the truth is not in him. This passage is evidently intended for "correction" to those Christians who are claiming to be free from the sin nature and who may have made themselves believe that they are free. A self-satisfied mind is not necessarily the mind of God.

In the same passage Christians are also warned against saying that they have not sinned as a fruit of the old nature: "If we say that we have not sinned, we make him a liar, and his word is not in us" (I John 1:10). Nothing could be more explicit. It is possible that a Christian may have been instructed to say that he has not sinned; but here is a word of "reproof," when he confronts the testimony of the Spirit of God. Again, this is not concerning some unsanctified class of Christians: it is concerning *all* Christians. To depart from the clear teaching of this great corrective passage is to make Him a "liar" and to disclose the fact that "his word is not in us."

The source of sin is, then, the sin nature, rather than the new divine nature. This important truth is pointed out in this same Epistle in a passage which primarily teaches that the Christian does not now *practice* sin as he did before he received the new divine nature, but which also teaches that sin cannot be traced to the divine nature as its *source*. "Not anyone that has been begotten of God practices sin, because his seed [the divine nature] in him abides, and he [with particular reference to the 'seed'] is not able to sin, because of God he [the 'seed'] has been begotten" (3:9, literal). It is evident that the new nature is that which has been begotten of God, and because of the presence of this nature the one in whom it dwells does not now practice sin as he did before he was saved, nor can sin ever be *produced* by the new nature which is from God. The passage does not teach that Christians do not sin, or even that *some* Christians do not sin; for there is no *class* of Christians in view, and what is here said is true of *all* who have been "begotten of God."

It is further taught in the Scriptures that, since there are two natures in the believer, there is a conflict between the new nature, through the Spirit, and the old nature through the flesh. "This I say then, Walk in the Spirit and ye shall not fulfil the lust of the flesh. For the flesh lusteth against the Spirit, and the Spirit against the flesh: and these are contrary the one to the other: so that [when walking by the Spirit] ye cannot do the things that ye [otherwise] would" (Galatians 5:16, 17). Another aspect of this truth is taken up at length in Romans 7:15 to 8:4. In this passage the old "I" is seen to be in active opposition to the new "I."

It is sometimes claimed of this passage that it refers to an experience in the Apostle's life *before* he was saved. This is open to serious question. No such conflict can Biblically be related to the life of Saul of Tarsus, nor to any other unregenerate man. Saul of Tarsus was not a "wretched man": he was a self-satisfied

Pharisee, living "in all good conscience" and "before the law blameless." It was only when he began to "delight in the law of God after the inward man" that this deeper conflict was experienced. So, also, the claim is sometimes made that this passage had to do only with Paul as a Jew under the law of Moses and so could not apply to any Gentile, since the law of Moses was not addressed to Gentiles. It is quite true that the law was not given to Gentiles. The primary purpose of this passage is not to set forth some distinguishing characteristic of a Jew under the law: it plainly represents a saint confronted with the impossibility of living according to the revealed will of God, not only because of the human impotence, but because of an active opposing principle in the "flesh." The law of Moses, if there referred to exclusively, it would seem, is referred to as an illustration of a clear statement of the mind and will of God. The mind and will of God for the believer under grace as has been seen, is infinitely more impossible to human strength than the law of Moses. So much the more are we found to be "wretched" men when attempting our present conflict in the "arm of the flesh." The "law" of God, as referred to in the New Testament, sometimes means His present will for His people rather than simply the "law of Moses." It is clear that the conflict in this passage is over "evil" and "good" in general terms, rather than over the law of Moses. If believers under grace are not in view in Romans seven, neither are they in Romans eight; for in passing from one chapter to the other there is no break in the development of the doctrine or its application.[1] Earlier in the context the law of Moses has been set aside (6:14; 7:1-6), and the new law of Christ (I Corinthians 9:21; Galatians 5:2; John 15:10), the "life in Christ Jesus" (8:2), or that which is produced *in* the believer by the *Spirit* (8:4), has come into view.

---

[1]In meeting this claim it has been pointed out that there is a particular crisis indicated by the words in 7:25, "I thank God through our Lord Jesus Christ." However this is not a word of thanksgiving for salvation: it is praise for deliverance from the reigning power of sin. And it is deliverance for one who could say: "So then with the mind I myself serve the law of God; but with the flesh the law of sin." This scarcely describes the experience of an unregenerate man.

No mention of the Spirit is made in this passage. It is therefore not a conflict between the Spirit and the "flesh": it is rather a conflict between the new "I" and the old "I." It is the new "I" — the regenerate man — isolated, for the time being, from the enabling power of the Spirit, and seen as confronting the whole law of God (v. 16), the unchanging "flesh" (v. 18), and the capacities of the new man (vs. 22, 23, 25). A vital question is raised — Can the regenerate man, apart from the Spirit, fulfil the whole will of God? The answer is clear. Though he "delight" in the law of God (in which no unregenerate man delights, see Romans 3:10-18; I Corinthians 2:14), he must discover the divinely provided power to live through the death of Christ (v. 25), and through the power of the Spirit (8:2). Apart from this there is only continued defeat (v. 24).

The passage, with some interpretations, is as follows: "For that which I [the old] do I [the new] allow not: for what I [the new] would, that do I [the old] not; but what I [the new] hate, that do I [the old]. If then I [the old] do that which I [the new] would not, I consent unto the law [or will of God for me] that it is good. Now then it is no more I [the new] that do it, but sin [the old] that dwelleth in me. For I know that in me [the old] (that is, in my flesh), dwelleth no good thing: for to will is present with me; but how to perform that which is good I find not. For the good that I [the new] would I [the old] do not: but the evil which I [the new] would not, that I [the old] do. Now if I [the old] do that I [the new] would not, it is no more I [the new] that do it, but sin [the old] that dwelleth in me. I find then a law [not a law of Moses], that, when I [the new] would do good, evil [the old] is present with me. For I delight in the law of God after the inward man: but I see another law in my members [the old], warring against the law of my mind [the new that delights in the law of God], and bringing me into captivity to the law of sin [the old] which is in my members. O wretched [Christian] man that I am! who shall deliver me from the body of this death?"

The answer to this great question and cry of distress with which the above passage closes is given in a following verse (8:2):

"For the law of the Spirit of life in Christ Jesus hath made me free from the law of sin and death." This is more than a deliverance from the law of Moses: it is the immediate deliverance from sin (the old) and death (its results, see Romans 6:23). The effect of this deliverance is indicated by the blessedness recorded in the eighth chapter as in contrast to the wretchedness recorded in the seventh chapter. It is all of the helpless and defeated "I" in the one case, and of the sufficient and victorious "I," by the Spirit, in the other. We are, then, to be delivered by the "law," or power, of the Spirit. But attention must be called to the fact, stated in 7:25, that it is "through Jesus Christ our Lord." We are delivered *by* the Spirit; but it is made righteously possible *through* Jesus Christ our Lord, because of our union with Him in His crucifixion, death, and burial.

THE BELIEVER'S DEATH WITH CHRIST

Substitution is the only reason assigned in the Bible for the death of Christ. He was taking the place of others. It was an infinite undertaking which accomplished infinite results. There is nothing more fundamental in a believer's understanding than that he apprehend to some degree just what the death of Christ wrought. There should be more teaching on this great theme. One result of the act of remembering the Lord's death in the breaking of bread is the deepening of the personal consciousness of the meaning and value of that death. It is noticeable that those Christians who are frequently exercised in spirit toward His death in the breaking of bread are most awake concerning the value of the sacrifice of Christ for them. The disciples met on the first day of the week to break bread (Acts 20:7). They knew the real desire of the Lord for them in this important matter and they knew the value of this ordinance in their own lives. A child of God should always be increasing in heart appreciation of his Saviour's finished work. Provision for this has been made in the faithful remembering of His death at His table.

Through His sufferings unto death the Son of God bore the penalty of our sins, making it righteously possible for a holy God to receive sinners into His saving grace without punishment for their sins. Sinners, because of His substitution for them, have only to *believe* and be saved. Men are now facing the one issue of personal trust in the Saviour, and are condemned only because of their failure to believe on the Son of God (John 3:18; II Corinthians 5:19). In like manner, a positive reality concerning the sin nature was accomplished for the believer in the death of Christ. By that death it has been made righteously possible for a holy God to take control of the old nature without any present judgments of that nature, and for the believer to be delivered from its power. By the death of Christ the *penalty* of sins committed was borne for all men, and the *power* of sin was judged and broken for the children of God. The accomplishment of all this was a problem of infinite dimensions; for sin is primarily against God and He alone can deal with it. The Bible pictures sin as seen from the divine standpoint. It also unfolds God's problem which was created by sin and records His exact manner and method of its solution.

The theme under consideration is concerned with the death of Christ as that death is related to the divine judgments of the sin nature in the child of God. The necessity for such judgments and the sublime revelation that these judgments are now fully accomplished for us is unfolded in Romans 6:1-10. This passage is the *foundation* as well as the *key* to the possibility of a "walk in the Spirit." Herein it is declared that Christians need not "continue in sin," but may "walk in newness of life." "Sin shall not have dominion over you," and we need no longer be the "bond-slaves to sin." To this end He hath wrought in the cross. How important in His eyes, then, is the quality of our daily life; for His death not only contemplated our eternal blessedness in the glory, but our present "walk" as well!

The old nature must be judged in order that God may be free to deal with it in the believer's daily life and apart from all judgments. What destruction would fall on the unsaved if God had to judge *them* for their sins before they could be saved! "O LORD, correct me, but with judgment; not in thine anger, lest thou bring me to nothing" (Jeremiah 10:24). How great is His mercy! He has already taken up the sin question and solved it for all men in the death of the Substitute. Because of this He can now save from the *penalty* of sin. Even so, to what lengths His mercy has gone since He has also entered into righteous judgments of our "old man"! And because of this He is now able to deliver His child from the *power* of sin. The "old man" is said to have been "crucified with him," and we are "dead with him," "buried with him" and are partaking in His resurrection life. All this, it is revealed, was to one great purpose, that "we also should walk in newness of life," even as Christ "was raised from the dead by the glory of the Father." What a deliverance and walk may be experienced since it is according to the *power* and *glory* of the resurrection! Resurrection, it may be added, is not the mere reversal of death; it is the introduction into the power and limitless boundaries of *eternal life*. In that new sphere and by that new power the Christian may now "walk."

The passage opens thus: "What shall we say then? Shall we continue in sin, that grace may abound? God forbid. How shall we, that are dead to sin [We who have died to sin. So, also, vs. 7, 8, 11; Colossians 2:20; 3:3], live any longer therein?"

In the preceding chapters of this Epistle salvation into *safety* has been presented. At the beginning of this passage the question of salvation into *sanctity* of daily life is taken up. This second aspect of salvation is provided only for the one who is already saved into *safety*. "Shall we [who are now saved and safe in grace] continue in sin?" It would not *become* us to do so, as the children of God, and it is not *necessary* for us to do so since we are now "dead to sin." But who is "dead to sin"? Is it true that any Christian ever *experienced* a death to sin? *Never was there one*. But the death which is mentioned in this passage is said to be accomplished for *every* believer. All Christians are here said to have died unto sin. A death which is all-inclusive could not be *experimental*. It is *positional*. God reckons *all* believers, as to their sin nature, to have died *in* Christ and *with* Christ; for only thus can they "walk in newness of life" as those who are "alive unto God." It is no longer *necessary* to sin. We cannot plead the power of a tendency over which we have no control.

We still have the tendency, and it is more than we can control; but God has provided the possibility of a complete victory and freedom both by judging the old nature and by giving us the presence and power of the Spirit. We are dependent upon God alone for any deliverance; but He could not deliver until He had first righteously judged our sin nature. This He has done and He has also given us the Spirit who is ever present and wholly able. Thus the necessity to sin is broken and we are free to move on another plane and in the power of His resurrection life.

Then follows the important explanation of the believer's present relation to the death of Christ as forming the grounds of his deliverance from the power of sin. First an outline is given (vs. 3, 4), and then the same truth is repeated, but more in detail (vs. 5-10). It is not within the scope of this discussion to consider the importance of a sacrament that purports to represent the truth of our death with Christ. Such, at best, is but the shadow of the substance. No ordinance performed by man can accomplish what is here described. Our baptism *into* Jesus Christ can be none other than the act of God in placing us *in* Christ (cf. Galatians 3:27). This evidently is our baptism into His body by the Spirit (I Corinthians 12:13); for in no other sense are we *all* "baptized into Jesus Christ." Being by the baptism of the Spirit vitally united and placed "*in Him*" we partake of what He *is*, and what He has *done*. He *is* the righteousness of God and the Scriptures teach that we are *made* the righteousness of *God in Him* (II Corinthians 5:21), and are *made* accepted *in the Beloved* (Ephesians 1:6). All this is true because we are "*in Him.*" So, also, He has substituted for us, and what He has *done* is reckoned unto us because we are "*in Him,*" — or because we are baptized into Jesus Christ. The argument in this passage is based on this vital union by which we are organically united to Christ through our baptism into His body: "Know ye not [Or are ye ignorant] that so many of us as were baptized into Jesus Christ were baptized into his death?" As certainly as we are "*in Him*" we partake of the *value* of His death. So, also the passage states: "Therefore we are buried with him by baptism into death" (cf. Colossians 2:12). Thus we are actually partakers of His crucifixion (v. 6), death (v. 8), burial (v. 4), and resurrection (vs. 4, 5, 8) and as essentially as we would partake had *we* been crucified, dead, buried and raised. Being baptized into Jesus Christ is the *substance* of which co-crucifixion, co-death, co-burial and co-resurrection are *attributes.* One is the *cause:* while the others are the *effects.* All this is unto the realization of one great divine purpose. "That like as Christ was raised up from the dead by the glory of the Father, even so we also should walk in newness of life," or by a new life principle. Our *"walk,"* then, is the divine objective. Christ died in our stead. The judgment belonged to us; but He became our Substitute. We are thus counted as co-partners in all that our Substitute did. What He did, forever satisfied the righteous demands of God against our "old man" and opened the way for a "walk" well pleasing to God (see II Corinthians 5:15).

As the passage proceeds, this truth of our co-partnership in Christ is presented again and with greater detail: "For if [as] we have been planted [conjoined, united, grown together, the word is used but once in the New Testament] together in the likeness [oneness, see Romans 8:3; Philippians 2:7] of his death, we shall be [now, and forever] also in the likeness of his resurrection." We are already conjoined to Christ by the baptism of the Spirit (I Corinthians 12:12, 13) which places us positionally beyond the judgments of sin and we are therefore free to enter the experience of the eternal power and victory of His resurrection. "Knowing this [because we know this] that our old man is [was] crucified with him [for the same divine purpose as stated before], that the body of sin might be destroyed [Our power of expression is through the body. This fact is used as a figure concerning the manifestation of sin. The body is not destroyed; but sin's power and means of expression may be disannulled. See v. 12], that henceforth we should not serve [be bond-slaves to] sin [the "old man"]. For he that is dead is freed [justified] from sin [they who have once died to sin, as we have in our Substitute, now stand free from its legal claims]. Now if we be dead with Christ [or, as we died with Christ], we believe we shall also live with him [not only in heaven, but *now.* There is as much certainty for the *life* in Him as there is certainty in the *death* in Him]: Knowing [or, because we know] that Christ being raised from the dead dieth no more; death hath no more dominion over him [We are thereby encouraged to believe as much concerning ourselves]. For in that he died, he died unto sin [the nature] once: but in that he liveth, he liveth unto God" (and so we may live unto God).

Such facts are recorded in the Scriptures concerning the meaning and value of the death of Christ and our present position in Him that we may be led to *believe* that it is all for us and is actually true of us *now*. Believing this, we will fearlessly claim our position in His boundless grace and dare to enter the life of victory.

Thus far in this passage nothing has been said touching any human obligation, nor has reference been made to any work of man. It is all the work of God for us, and the conclusion of this great passage is to the effect that it is His plan and provision that we should know that we have already provided for us a deliverance from the bond-servitude to sin. Based on this knowledge gained from His Word concerning all that God has done in Christ, an injunction immediately follows which presents our responsibility: "Likewise reckon ye also yourselves to be dead indeed unto sin, but alive unto God through Jesus Christ our Lord." We are not exhorted to reckon the *sin nature* to be dead; but we are exhorted to reckon *ourselves* to be dead unto it. Did the death of Christ literally destroy the power of the "old man" so that we can have no disposition to sin? No, for the passage goes on to state: "Let not sin therefore reign in your mortal body, that ye should obey it in the lusts thereof." Evidently, then, the "old man" will remain active, apart from sufficient control. The union with Christ has provided a *possible* deliverance; but it must be entered into and claimed by such human acts of faith as are expressed in the word "reckon," and the additional words which follow in the passage: "But yield yourselves unto God, as those that are alive from the dead, and your members as instruments of righteousness unto God. For sin [the nature] shall not have dominion over you: for ye are not under the law [which provides no power for its fulfilment], but under grace" (which provides the sufficient Substitute and limitless enablement of the Spirit of God).

Every provision has been made. "Let not sin therefore reign in your mortal body, that ye should obey it in the lusts thereof." Who can measure the truth that is compressed in the one word "therefore"? It refers to *all* of the divine undertaking in the death of Christ by which we have been conjoined to Christ in order that we may receive the eternal values of His crucifixion, death, burial and resurrection. All this was accomplished for us before we were born. "Therefore," because of all this that is now accomplished and provided, we have limitless encouragement to enter into His plan and purpose for our deliverance. Faith, which believes the victory to be possible because it reckons the "old man" to have been judged, is the normal result of such a revelation. We are nowhere enjoined to *enact* His crucifixion, death, burial and resurrection; but we are encouraged by the revelation of what has been done to *reckon* the divine requirements for our deliverance from the "old man" to have been met perfectly and to believe that, because of this, we can now "walk in newness of life."

Will any Scripture justify the claim that some Christians have died to sin as a personal experience?

Several New Testament passages refer to the believer as being already dead. None of these, however, refer to an *experience:* they refer rather to a *position* into which the believer has been brought through his union with Jesus Christ in His death. "Wherefore if ye be dead with Christ" (Colossians 2:20); "For ye are dead [ye died], and your life is hid with Christ in God" (Colossians 3:3); "I am crucified with Christ" (Galatians 2:20); "But God forbid that I should glory, save in the cross of our Lord Jesus Christ, by whom the world is crucified unto me, and I unto the world" (Galatians 6:14); "And they that are Christ's have crucified the flesh with the affections and lusts" (Galatians 5:24). In the last passage, as in the others, reference is made to some thing that is accomplished in *all* those who are Christ's. It could not, therefore, refer to some experience, the result of a special or particular sanctity on the part of a *few*. These passages, since they refer to all believers, can have but one meaning: in their union with Christ the "flesh with the affections and lusts" has *positionally* been crucified. The word crucify as related to believers is always in the *past*, implying the judicial fact and not a spiritual experience. The believer may *"mortify"* which means to reckon to be dead; but he is never called upon to *crucify*. Even mortifying is possible only by the enabling power of the Spirit. "But if ye through the Spirit do mortify the deeds of the body, ye shall live" (Romans 8:13). We are plainly told the crucifixion is accomplished once for all. In view of this divine accomplishment, the child of God is to "reckon," "yield," "mortify" (count to be dead), "put off," "let," "put away," "take unto you the whole armour of God," "set your affection on things above," "put on the new man which is renewed in knowledge after the image of him that created him," "deny himself," "abide" in Christ, "fight," "run the race," "walk in love," "walk in the Spirit," "walk in the light," "walk in newness of life." Such is the human responsibility toward that deliverance which God has provided *through* the death of His Son and proposes now to accomplish *by* the Spirit.

The divine objective, then, in all that is recorded in Romans 6:1-10 is that we may "walk in newness of life." God has met every demand of His holiness in accomplishing for us, through Christ, all the judgments against the sin nature that He could ever demand. It is recorded for us to *understand* and *believe*. "Knowing this," or, because we know this, we are justified in our confidence that we may "walk in newness of life," by the enabling power of the Spirit. What rest, peace and victory would be the portion of the children of God if they really did *know* that the "old man" *was* crucified with Christ and so, on the divine side, it is made possible for them to live where sin's power and manifestation may be constantly disannulled!

THE SUMMARIZING SCRIPTURE

The whole doctrinal statement concerning a possible deliverance from the bond-servitude to sin, contained in Romans 6:1

to 8:4, is summarized and concluded in the last two verses of the context (8:3, 4). In these two verses seven factors which enter into the revelation concerning a possible victory over sin, and which have been the subjects of discussion in the whole context, are mentioned again as a consummation of all that has gone before. The seven factors are:

1. "The law" (8:3) which represents the righteous will of God. Not limited to the law of Moses (see 6:14; 7:4, 25) which passed away (7:1-4; II Corinthians 3:1-18; Galatians 3:24, 25). It includes that which the Spirit produces *in* the one who is spiritual (8:4; Galatians 5:22, 23). The attempt to secure perfect righteousness through obedience, in mere human strength, to *any* precepts will always fail. Grace provides that its heaven-high standards shall be realized through the energizing power of the Spirit.

2. "The weakness of the flesh" (8:3), or the utter inability of human resources in the presence of the heavenly requirements (7:14-21; John 15:5).

3. "Sin in the flesh" (8:3). That in the flesh which is different from "weakness": it is *opposed* to the Spirit (7:14-23; Galatians 5:17).

4. Christ came "in the likeness of sinful flesh" (8:3). He took the place of vital union with the sinner (6:5, 10, 11); but did not become a sinner, or partake of the sin nature (Hebrews 4:15; 7:26).

5. "And for sin, condemned [judged] sin in the flesh" (8:3). Thus He met every claim of the righteousness of God against the "old man" (6:10; 7:25).

6. "That the righteousness of the law [see 7:4, 22, 25] might be fulfilled in us" (8:4): never to be fulfilled *by* us (6:4, 14; 7:4, 6). It is the "fruit of the Spirit."

7. "Who walk not after the flesh, but after the Spirit" (8:4). Such is the human condition for a victorious "walk." It must be by the Spirit (6:11-22).

Full provisions are made through the divine judgment of the "flesh" and the "old man" for the spiritual life of every Christian, even the fulfilling of the whole will of God *in* us by the Spirit. But these provisions become effective only to those who "walk not after the flesh, but after the Spirit." We have clear revelations and instructions from God and it is perilous to neglect or confuse these, or to fail in the exact responsibilities committed to us.

II. THE DIVINE REMEDY

The divine method of dealing with the sin nature in the believer is by direct and unceasing *control* over that nature by the indwelling Spirit. This it may be stated, is one of the most important undertakings of the Spirit *in* and *for* the believer. He proposes both to *control* the old nature and to *manifest* the new.

TWO THEORIES

Two general theories are held as to the divine method of dealing with the sin nature in believers. One suggests that the old nature is *eradicated,* either when one is saved, or at some subsequent crisis of experience and spiritual blessing, and the quality of the believer's life depends, therefore, on the *absence* of the disposition to sin.[1] The other theory contends that the old nature abides so long as the Christian is in this body and that the quality of life depends on the immediate and constant control over the "flesh" by the indwelling Spirit of God, and this is made possible through the death of Christ. In both of these propositions there is a sincere attempt to realize the full victory in daily life which is promised to the child of God. One theory begins with a very high assumption and then immediately modifies and qualifies its claims until it approaches the level of actual *experience.* The other begins with a full recognition of the human limitation and then discovers so much in the death of Christ and in the presence, purpose and power of

---

[1]Eradication beliefs are not well defined. There is marked disagreement among its supporters as to the lengths to which they are willing to press the theory. It is not within the purpose of this discussion to present the various shades and modifications that are held of this theory: rather the extreme logical results of the theory are stated in order that the most obvious contrasts may be drawn between these two entirely different principles of Christian living.

the Spirit that the possible results are boundless. The life that is delivered from the bond-servitude to sin is the *objective* in each theory. It is therefore only a question as to which is the plan and method of God in the realization. Both theories cannot be true, for they are contradictory. In seeking to determine which of the two is according to the Word of God, it may be stated:

First, Eradication is not the divine method of dealing with the believer's difficulties.

There are three outstanding reasons why the Christian must depend wholly on the Spirit of God. He faces the "world, the flesh and the devil." He is not delivered from the low standards of the world into the high standards of the heavenly citizen by the *eradication* of the world. He is not delivered from his conflict with the enemy by the *eradication* of Satan. These victories are said to be gained by the direct and constant power of God. It is reasonable in the light of these facts to conclude that it is not the divine method to deal with the "flesh," or "sin" by *eradication*. Of what real value is eradication in the conflict with the sin nature if it cannot be claimed in the conflict with the world and with the devil?

Second, Eradication is not according to human experience.

It may be according to the immodest human assumption of a few; but most of its defenders dare not claim complete freedom from sin, but they have invented various theories by which they seek to account for their sin. One theory is to the effect that their sin is the sin of an unfallen being, such as Adam was before he sinned. Concerning this claim it may be said that we are not saved into conformity to the first Adam: we are now *in Christ* and saved into conformity to the Last Adam. If this theory were true, the first sin committed by any person in that innocent state would result in a fall as far reaching and serious as was the effect of Adam's sin on his own nature and on his relation to God.

Again, some fancy a distinction between their fallen nature and the human nature, and they claim that they sin from the human nature even though the fallen nature is eradicated. Such a theory finds no basis in the Scriptures.

God has a better way of preventing sin, which is clearly revealed. It is free from bold assumption because it makes "no provision for the flesh" and depends only upon the power of the Spirit. The claim of eradication is foreign to the experience of the most spiritual saints in this and past generations. There is no example of eradication in the Word of God.

Third, Eradication is not according to Revelation.

In the Word of God we have "instruction," "correction," and "reproof." By these we must determine our conclusions rather than by any impression of the mind, or by analyzing any person's experience whatsoever. The Bible teaches:

(1), All believers are warned against the assumptions of the eradication theory: "If we say that we have no sin [nature], we deceive ourselves, and the truth is not in us" (I John 1:8).

(2), The Spirit has come to be our Deliverer and the whole Bible teaching concerning His presence, purpose and power is manifestly meaningless if our victory is to be by another means altogether. For this reason the eradication theory makes little place for the Person and work of the Spirit.

(3), The Spirit delivers by an unceasing conflict. "The flesh [which includes the old nature] lusteth against the Spirit, and the Spirit against the flesh: and these are contrary the one to the other: so that [when walking by the Spirit] ye cannot do the things that ye [otherwise] would" (Galatians 5:17, cf. James 4:5). So, also, in Romans 7:15-24, and 8:2, the *source* of sin in the believer is said to be the sin nature working through the flesh, and the victory is by the superior power of the Spirit. The extreme teachings of the eradication theory are to the effect that a Christian will have no disposition to sin tomorrow and thus the theory prompts one to an alarming disregard for true watchfulness and reliance upon the power of God. The Bible teaches that the latent source of sin remains and, should the "walk in the Spirit" cease, there will be an immediate return to the "desires" and "lusts" of the flesh. So long as "by the

Spirit ye are walking, ye shall not fulfil the lust of the flesh." We are all creatures of habit and may become increasingly *adapted* to the walk in the Spirit. We store knowledge through experience as well. Thus the walk in the "flesh" may cease at a given time; but the *ability* to walk after the "flesh" abides.

In this aspect of it, true spirituality means, for the time, not wishing to sin (Philippians 2:13); but this does not imply the eradication of the ability to sin: it means rather that, because of the energizing power of God, a complete victory for the present time is possible. It remains true that we always need Him completely. He said, "Apart from me ye can do nothing" (John 15:5). Because the "infection" of sin is always in us, we need every moment "the conquering counteraction of the Spirit." The "walk" in the Spirit is divinely enabled at every step of the way.

(4), The divine provisional dealings with the "flesh" and the "old man" have not been unto eradication. God has wrought on an infinite scale in the death of His Son that the way might be made whereby we may "walk in newness of life." The manner of this walk is stated in such injunctions as "reckon," "yield," "let not," "put off," "mortify," "abide": yet not one of these injunctions would have the semblance of meaning under the eradication theory. The Scriptures do not counsel us to "reckon" the nature to be dead: it urges us to "reckon" ourselves to be dead unto *it*.

(5), The teachings of the eradicationists are based on a false interpretation of Scripture concerning the present union of the believer with Christ in His death. That in the Bible which is held to be *positional* and existing only in the mind and reckoning of God, and which is accomplished once for all for every child of God, is supposed to mean an *experience* in the daily life of a *few* who dare to class themselves as those who are free from the disposition to sin.

(6), The conclusions of the doctrine of eradication are based on false teachings concerning the Bible use of the word "flesh." The advocates of this teaching do not understand that the word "flesh" refers to *all*, — spirit, soul and body, — of the natural man, and, were it possible, the removal of the sin nature would not dispose of all the problems created by the limitations of the "flesh." "In me (that is, in my flesh), dwelleth no good thing." The "flesh" must, therefore remain so long as the "earthen vessel," the "body of our humiliation" remains. Certainly the body is not eradicated.

(7), Eradication teaching is more concerned with human experience than with the revelation of God. It has always been content to analyze experience and attempt to prove its conclusions by such analysis. That which is a normal experience of deliverance by the power of the Spirit may easily be supposed to be an evidence of "sinless perfection," "entire sanctification" and "eradication." A human supposition can never take the place of the divine revelation.

The two theories are irreconcilable. We are either to be delivered by the abrupt removal of all tendency to sin and so no longer need the enabling power of God to combat the power of sin, or we are to be delivered by the immediate and constant power of the indwelling Spirit. The Bible evidently teaches the latter.

WHAT IS SPIRITUALITY?

The third condition, then, upon which one may be spiritual, is a definite reliance upon the Spirit, which is a "walk by means of the Spirit." Such a reliance upon the Spirit is imperative because of the impossible heavenly calling, the opposing power of Satan, and the continued presence of the "flesh" with its Adamic nature. We cannot meet tomorrow's issues today. The walk is step by step and this demands a *constant* appropriation of the power of God. The Christian life is never likened to a balloon ascension in which we might go up once for all and have no trouble or temptation again. It is a *"walk,"* a *"race,"* a *"fight."* All this speaks of continuation. The fight of faith is that of continuing the attitude of reliance upon the Spirit. To those who thus walk with God, there is open a door into "fellowship with the Father and with his Son" and into a life of fruit-bearing and service with every spiritual manifestation to the glory of God.

What, then, is true spirituality? It is the unhindered manifestations of the indwelling Spirit. There are in all, seven of these manifestations. These blessed realities are all provided for in the presence and power of the Spirit and will be normally produced by the Spirit in the Christian who is not grieving the Spirit, but has confessed every *known* sin; who is not quenching the Spirit, but is yielded to God; and who is walking in the Spirit by an attitude of dependence upon His power alone. Such an one is spiritual because He is Spirit-filled. The Spirit is free to fulfil in him all the purpose and desire of God for him. There is nothing in daily life and service to be desired beyond this. "But thanks be unto God, which giveth us the victory through our Lord Jesus Christ."

CHAPTER 7

AN ANALOGY AND THE CONCLUSION

I. An Analogy

THE BIBLE TREATS our deliverance from the bond-servitude to sin as a distinct form of salvation, and there is an analogy between this and the more familiar aspect of salvation which is from the guilt and penalty of sin. In the first five chapters of the letter to the Romans we have presented our salvation from the guilt and penalty of sin into justification and security through the redemption that is in Christ. Beginning with chapter six, a new question is raised: "Shall we [who have been saved into safety] continue in sin?" The major portion of three chapters, as has been stated, is then devoted to a statement of the facts and conditions of salvation from the reigning *power* of sin in the daily life of the child of God. The analogy between these two aspects of salvation may be considered in five particulars:

FIRST, THE ESTATE OF THE ONE WHO NEEDS TO BE SAVED —

a, From the penalty of sin.

The Word of God presents an extended description of the estate of the unregenerate in their need of salvation from the guilt and penalty of sin. They are said to be "lost," "condemned," and spiritually "dead"; "there is none righteous, no, not one"; "all have sinned and come short of the glory of God." But back of all this is the revelation that in themselves they are helpless and without power to alter or improve their condition. Their only hope is to depend completely on Another for His saving power and grace. "Believe on the Lord Jesus Christ and thou shalt be saved."

134

b, From the power of sin.

In like manner the Scriptures reveal the estate of the regenerate in relation to the *power* of the sin nature, to be that of impotence and helplessness: "For I know that in me (that is, in my flesh) dwelleth no good thing"; "I find then a law, that, when I would do good, evil is present with me." The hope of the child of God in salvation from the *power* of sin is also a complete dependence upon the power and grace of Another. "For the law of the Spirit of life in Christ Jesus hath made me free from the law of sin and death." "If by the Spirit ye are walking, ye shall not fulfil the lust of the flesh."

SECOND, THE DIVINE OBJECTIVE AND IDEAL IN SALVATION —

a, From the penalty of sin.

The greatest possible contrast exists between what an unregenerate person is before he is saved, and that estate to which he is brought in the saving power of God. Eternity will hardly suffice to give opportunity to discover the manifold marvels of His saving grace, "When we see him, we shall be like him." Even now "are we the sons of God." We are to be "conformed to the image of his Son."

b, From the power of sin.

So, also, the Christian, in the purpose of God, is to find a perfect victory through Jesus Christ, and by the power of the Spirit. "I therefore, the prisoner of the Lord, beseech you that you walk worthy of the vocation wherewith ye are called." "Grieve not the Spirit." "Quench not the Spirit." "Walk in the light." "Abide in me."

THIRD, SALVATION IS OF GOD ALONE —

a, From the penalty of sin.

Salvation *must* be of God alone; for every aspect of it is beyond human power and strength. Of the many great miracles which taken together constitute salvation from the guilt and penalty of sin, not one of them could even be understood, let alone be accomplished, by man. "It is the power of God unto salvation"; "That he might be the justifier of him which believeth."

b, From the power of sin.

It is equally true that the believer is helpless to deliver himself from the power of sin. God alone can do it, and He proposes to do it according to the revelation contained in His Word. There is no power in man to deliver from "the world, the flesh and the devil." "If by the Spirit ye are walking, ye shall not fulfil the lust of the flesh"; "It is God which worketh in you both to will and to do of his good pleasure"; "The law of the Spirit of life in Christ Jesus hath made me free from the law of sin and death"; "Finally, my brethren, be strong in the Lord, and in the power of his might"; "Through Jesus Christ our Lord."

FOURTH, GOD CAN SAVE ONLY BY, AND THROUGH, THE CROSS —

a, From the penalty of sin.

There would not be a sinner left to save, if God had to deal with the sin question in us, as to its guilt and penalty, at the moment He would exercise saving grace. It is only that He has *already* dealt with the penalty of sin in the death of Christ that He can save the sinner apart from consuming judgments. Now, the sinner has only to *believe* that such saving grace is open to him through the Son of God. The Lord Jesus suffered unto death *"for"* our sins. "He bore our sins in his body on the tree"; "He was delivered for our transgressions"; "Because we thus judge, that if one died for all, then all died" (in the One). By this death He so perfectly met the condemnation of sin for us that God is now free even to justify any sinner without penalty or condemnation. A moral hindrance in a sinner's life is no longer an issue in his salvation. By the death of His Son, God has rendered Himself free to save the chief of sinners. In such salvation He is *righteous* and *just* because the Lord Jesus has suffered *for* our sins.

b, From the power of sin.

There could not be any salvation for the Christian from the *power* of sin if God had not first taken the "old man" into judgment. Our condition would be hopeless if God had first to judge the sin nature in us before He could take control in our lives. He has already judged the "old man" by our co-crucifixion, co-death, and co-burial with Christ. The Lord not only suffered *for* our sins. He also died *unto* sin. He suffered under the penalty *for* our sins: He also died *unto* our sin nature. "For in that he died unto sin once." "Knowing this, that our old man was crucified with him." Because Christ has died unto sin, God is righteously free to take control of the "flesh," and the Adamic nature, and exercise His power for our salvation from the bond-servitude to sin; exactly as He is righteously free to save the unregenerate from the penalty of sin because Christ has met every judgment for the sinner.

FIFTH, SALVATION IS BY FAITH —

a, From the penalty of sin.

Since salvation is always and only a work of God, the only relation man can sustain to it is that of expectation toward the One who alone can undertake and accomplish it. Salvation from the guilt and penalty of sin is wrought for us the *moment* we believe. It is conditioned on the *act* of faith. Men are not saved, or kept saved, from the consequences of sins because they *continue* their faith. Saving faith, as related to the first aspect of salvation, is an *act* of faith. We are saved by grace through faith.

b, From the power of sin.

Salvation unto sanctity of daily life is equally a work of God, and the only relation the child of God can sustain to it is an *attitude* of expectation toward the One who alone is able. There should be an adjustment of the life and will to God, and this salvation must then be claimed by faith; but in this case it is an *attitude* of faith. We are saved from the power of sin *as* we believe. The one who has been justified by an *act* of faith must now *live* by faith. There are a multitude of sinners for whom Christ has died who are not now saved. On the divine side, everything has been provided, and they have only to enter by faith into His saving grace as it is for them in Jesus Christ. Just so, there are a multitude of saints whose sin nature has been perfectly judged and every provision made on the divine side for a life of victory and glory to God who are not now realizing a life of victory. They have only to enter by faith into the saving grace from the power and dominion of sin. This is the reality of a "walk," a "race," a "warfare." It is a *constant* attitude. We are to "fight the good fight of faith." Sinners are not saved until they trust the Savior, and saints are not victorious until they trust the Deliverer. God has made this *possible* through the cross of His Son. Salvation from the power of sin must be claimed by faith.[1]

The Spirit, when saving from the reigning power of sin does not set aside the personality of the one He saves. He takes possession of the faculties and powers of the individual. It is the power of God acting through the human faculties of the will, emotions, desires and disposition. The experience of the believer who is being empowered is only that of a consciousness of his own power of choice, his own feelings, desires and disposition as related to his own self. The strength which he possesses is "in the Lord and in the power of his might."

---

[1]Discussing this aspect of this same analogy, Bishop Moule, of England, writes: "The first case is in its nature one and single: an admission, an incorporation. The second is in its nature progressive and developing: the discovery, advancing with the occasion for it, of the greatness of the resources of Christ for life. The latter *may*, not *must*, thus include one great crisis in consciousness, one particular spiritual act. It is much more certain to include many starting-points, critical developments, marked advances. The act of self-surrendering faith in the power of Christ for inward cleansing of the will and affections may be, and often indeed it is, *as it were* a new conversion, a new 'effectual calling.' But it is sure, if the man knows himself in the light of Christ, to be followed by echoes and reiterations to the end; not mere returns to the beginnings from the old level (certainly it is not the plan of God that it should be so), but definite out-growths due to new discovery of personal need and sin, and of more than corresponding 'riches' in Christ. With each such advance the sacred promise of *Fullness of the Spirit* will be received with holy and happy realization." *"Outlines of Christian Doctrine,"* page 199.

II. THE CONCLUSION

Because thus far this discussion has dealt primarily with the theory, or doctrine of the spiritual life, the addition of a few practical suggestions may not be amiss.

Since a life in the power of the Spirit depends upon a *continuous* attitude of reckoning and appropriation, it is important for most Christians to have a time of definite dealing with God in which they examine their hearts in the matter of sin and their yieldedness, and in which they acknowledge both their insufficiency and His sufficiency by the Spirit. There, at that time, they may claim His power and strength to supplant their weakness. The Bible makes no rules as to time or conditions. It is the individual child, in all the latitude of his own personality, dealing with his *Father*.

Spirituality is not a future ideal: it is to be experienced *now*. The vital question is, "Am I walking in the Spirit *now?*" Answer to this question should not depend on the presence or absence of some unusual manifestation of the supernatural. Much of life will be lived in the uneventful commonplace; but, even there, we should have the conviction that we are right with God and in His unbroken fellowship. "Beloved, if our hearts condemn us not, then have we confidence toward God" (I John 3:21). Likewise, we should not mistake worn nerves, physical weakness or depression for unspirituality. Many times sleep is more needed than prayer, and physical recreation than heart searching.

Be it remembered, too, that His provisions are always *perfect;* but our entrance into these provisions is often *imperfect.* There is doubtless a too general reference to human attitudes and actions in relation to God as being *"absolute"*: such as *"absolute* surrender," *"absolute* consecration," and *"absolute* devotion." If there are well-defined conditions upon which we may be spiritual, let us remember that, from the standpoint of the Infinite God, our compliance with those conditions is often *imperfect.* What He provides and bestows is in the fullest divine perfection; but our adjustment is human and therefore is usually subject to improvement. The *fact* of our possible deliverance, which depends upon Him alone, does not change. We shall have as much at any time as we make it possible for Him to bestow.

Normally, the spiritual Christian will be occupied with effective service for his Lord. This is not a rule. We need only to know that we are yielded and ready to do whatever He may choose. To "rest in the Lord" is one of the essential victories in a spiritual life. "Come ye apart and rest awhile." We are just as spiritual when resting, playing, sleeping or incapacitated, if it is His will for us, as we are when serving.

The spiritual life is not passive. Too often it is thus misjudged and because of the fact that one, to be spiritual, must cease from self-effort in the direction of spiritual attainments and learn to live and serve by the power God has provided. True spirituality knows little of "quietism." It is life more active, enlarged and vital because it is energized by the limitless power of God. Spirit-filled Christians are quite apt to be physically exhausted at the close of the day. They are weary *in* the work, but not weary *of* the work.

The Spirit-filled life is never free from temptations; but "God is faithful, who will not suffer you to be tempted above that ye are able: but will with the temptation also make a way to escape, that ye may be able to bear it." The plain teaching of this promise, in harmony with all Scripture on this subject, is that temptations which are "common to man" come to us all, but there is a divinely provided way of escape. The child of God does not need to yield to temptation. There is always the *possibility* of sin; but never the *necessity*.

It has been well said that spiritual believers are honored with warfare in the front line trenches. There the fiercest pressure of the enemy is felt. But they are also privileged to witness the enemy's crushing defeat; so abundant is the power of God, and thus highly is the spiritual believer honored.

Living in unrealities is a source of hindrance to spirituality. Anything that savors of a "religious pose" is harmful. In a very particular sense the one who has been changed from the natural to the spiritual sometimes needs to be changed to a naturalness again, — meaning, of course, a naturalness of manner and life. The true spiritual life presents a latitude sufficient to allow us to live very close to all classes of people without drawing us from God. Spirituality hinders sin, but should never hinder the friendship and confidence of sinners (Luke 15:1). Who can see the failures of others more than the one who has spiritual vision? And because of this fact, who needs more the divine power to keep him from becoming critical, with all that follows with it? We need to study most carefully the adaptation practiced by the Apostle Paul as revealed in I Corinthians 9:19-22. If our kind of spirituality makes Christ unattractive to others, it needs some drastic changes. May God save His children from assuming a holy tone of the voice, a holy somberness of spirit, a holy expression of the face, or a holy garb (if by the garb they wish to appear holy). True spirituality is an inward adorning. It is most simple and natural and should be a delight and attraction to all.

It will not do to *impersonate* ideals or to *imitate* others. Just here is the great danger in analyzing experiences. Some are so easily induced to try to imitate someone else. That which gives us our priceless distinctiveness is our own personality, and we cannot please Him more than by being what He designed us to be. Some Christians are disposed to "traffic in unlived truth"; repeating pious phrases the truth of which they have never really experienced. This must always grieve the Spirit.

We are dealing always with our Father. Too often the walk in the Spirit is thought to be a mechanical thing. We are not dealing with a machine: we are dealing with the most loving and tender-hearted Father in all the universe. The deepest secret of our walk is just to *know Him*, and so to believe in His Father-heart that we can cry out our failures on His loving breast, if need be, or speak plainly to Him in thanksgiving for every victory. When we know the consolation and relief of such communion we shall have less occasion to trouble any one else. It is ours to tell Him just what we feel, just how bad we are at heart, and even our darkest unbelief. To do this only opens our hearts to Him for His blessed light and strength. Separation from close-up communion is the first thing that we should fear, and the "first aid" in every spiritual accident is the simple act of telling Him everything. Having made our confession, we should reckon our forgiveness and restoration fully accomplished and immediately take our place in His fellowship and grace.

The teaching that "the bird with the broken pinion never soars so high again" is most unscriptural. Through the sacrifice of Christ, no penalty because of sin remains for saint or sinner. Rather "the bird with a broken pinion may higher soar again"; but there should be no complacency with failure and defeat.

We are never wonderful saints of whom God may justly be proud: we are His little children, immature and filled with foolishness, with whom He is endlessly patient and on whom He has been pleased to set all His infinite heart of love. He is wonderful. We are not.

Believe what is written. Remember the vital words of Romans 6:6, 9: "Knowing this," or "because we know this." We are always justified in acting on good evidence. Where is there a safer word of testimony than the imperishable Word of our God? From that Word we *know* that God has provided a finished judgment for our sins and for our sin, and that the way is open for an overflowing life in the power of the blessed Spirit. We *know* that such a life is His loving purpose for us. Ours is to *believe* His unfailing promise. So far from imposing on Him by claiming His grace, to fail to claim *all* that His love would bestow will hurt Him more than all else.

We need give no direct attention to the increase of our faith. Faith grows as we contemplate the faithfulness of God. Count His Word to be true when He says, "My grace is sufficient for thee." So count on every provision and promise of God.

True spirituality is a reality. It is *all* of the manifestations of the Spirit in and through the one in whom He dwells. He manifests in the believer the life which is Christ. He came not to reveal Himself but to make Christ real *to* the heart, and *through* the heart, of man. Thus the Apostle Paul could write: "For this cause I bow by knees unto the Father of our Lord Jesus Christ, of whom the whole family in heaven and earth is named, that he would grant you, according to the riches of his glory, to be strengthened with might by his Spirit in the inner man; that Christ may dwell in your hearts by faith; that ye, being rooted and grounded in love, may be able to comprehend with all saints what is the breadth, and length, and depth, and height; and to know the love of Christ, which passeth knowledge, that ye might be filled with all the fulness of God. Now unto him that is able to do exceeding abundantly above all that we ask or think, according to the power that worketh in us, unto him be glory in the church by Christ Jesus throughout all ages, world without end. Amen."

INDEX OF SUBJECTS

145

INDEX OF SCRIPTURE TEXTS

We want to hear from you. Please send your comments about this book to us in care of zreview@zondervan.com. Thank you.

ZONDERVAN®

GRAND RAPIDS, MICHIGAN 49530 USA

ZONDERVAN.COM/
AUTHORTRACKER